MW01147607

Las nalgas de JLO

JLO'S Booty

The Best + Most Notorious Calumnas + Other Writings by The FIRST CHICANA columnist in TEXAS 1995-2005

Bárbara Renaud González

AZTLAN LIBRE PRESS • SAN ANTONIO, TEJAS

First Edition

Text copyright © 2017 by Bárbara Renaud González

Cover artwork copyright © 2017 by Cruz Ortiz

Special thanks to Machete Creative for their design/layout work
and Raquel Elizondo and David Cavazos for their
proofreading and editorial support.

Library of Congress Control Number: 2016963517
ISBN 978-0-9897782-3-7

1. Chicana Literature 2. Mexican American Journalism
3. Chicana Feminism 4. Chicana/o Studies
5. Literary Critique 6. Texas History 7. Politics

TABLE OF CONTENTS

WHY THIS BOOK MATTERS   5
DISCLAIMER—PA' QUE NO CHI...   7
DEDICATION TO THE INNOCENT AND THE
    ONE WHO IS GUILTY   9

I. THEY SAY I'M NO LADY

Have You Seen Peach?   17
Ay, Henry   18
Brown Men Can't Run   21
The Ultimate Taco Diet   24
Cerveza-Time!   27
Mejor Puto Que Joto   31
The Ashes of Lent   34
When Love is the Color Blue/The Police   37
El Mayor, B.C. (Before Castro)   39
Column Photo   42
Armed and Dangerous   43
Los Dropouts   46
Los Hermanos Briseño   49
The Suntan Club   52
Muchachitas   55
The Car Gods   58
Dan Morales, Affirmative Action Baby   61
Me and Kobe in the Back Seat   64
A Nation Addicted   67
Column Photo   70
Los Regalos   71
We Must Search the American Soul to Find the
    Mexican Conscience   74
Texas Governor, No Amigo   78

II. No Te Dejes/My Line in the Sand

Three Thousand Polkitas   83
Let's Party! It's 1999   85
The Water Gods of San Antonio   88
White Fear of a Brown Nation: Challenging Huntington   92
The Education of the Heart   97
The Forgetting of Alberto R. Gonzales   114

III. La Familia

El Borracho   119
Pass The Turkey   121
I Am My Mother's Hopes...and Fears   123
Remember Mariachis at My Funeral   126
A Confession/The Priest   129
Drugs in the Family   137
The Land of Barbacoa   141

IV. Mexico and Chile (The Country)

All She Wanted Was a Kiss   147
Pass the Salsa and la Conciencia   149
Blaming the Immigrant/Guanajuato, Gto., México   153
Immigrants Have a Story to Tell Us   158
La Cola del Mundo, Santiago de Chile   160
The Evangelicals, Santiago de Chile   163
Regresé de Mis Viajes: Seeking Pablo Neruda,
    Isla Negra, Chile   167

V. Pray For Us Women

A Christmas Story   175
For María Felix: Watching Juana Rooster on
   Sunday Afternoons   177
María Antonietta Berriozábal/Guardian Angel
   of San Antonio   181
Pray For Us Women   185
Count Me In   188

VI. Write Like It's Your Last Day on Earth/Reviews

The Secret of Bleach   193
To My Unborn Daughter: Tejana Poetry   194
José Antonio Burciaga/Spilling the Beans   197
Eduardo Galeano/The Truth Be Told: Eduardo Galeano
   Dispels Myths of History   202
Column Photo   206
Gloria Anzaldúa/This Bridge We Call Home   207
Daniela Rossell/Ricas y Famosas   210
Denise Chávez/Loving Pedro Infante   214
Alma Guillermoprieto/Looking for History: Dispatches
   from Latin America   217
The Targeting of Chicano!   220

VII. Forget the War, So We Can Remember It

Dear John,   239
The Cantina at the Alamo   241
Why We Can't Forget the Alamo   243
The Popcorn War   245

The Anniversary of the Chicano Moratorium   248
Daddy and the War   250
Peace   256
Don't Forgive Me, Don't Forget Me: The Grief of Carlos
    Arredondo Who Lost His Son in Iraq   260

VIII. Las Nalgas de JLo/JLo's Booty

Twilight of the Summer Share   267
My Picture as a Calumnista   268
Todas Somos Gloria: The Story of Gloria Trevi   271
Selena and Cisneros   274
Las Nalgas de JLo/JLo's Booty   276

A-diosa-tion: If you must know about 9/11   279
Afterword   283
Epigram   285
Original Published Titles   287

WHY THIS BOOK MATTERS

Bárbara Renaud González's style of journalism and prose provides a model for writing about issues necessary to re-generate social, political and intellectual life in this century. Her disciplined research is combined with a huge, curious heart about humanity and the resources from deep within the Chicana/o experience. Her informed voice combines colloquial expression and a political minority point of view, with a contemporary critical eye. These qualities lend themselves to speak of the hard issues we must relate to if we are to come any further from being a silent (silenced) majority, to becoming an active voice of political agency.

Issues concerning minorities, migration politics, the environment, the re-imagination of democratic power and policy, the valorization of languages and cultures are not only relevant for Chicanas/os, but crave attention as new *mestizo* cultures emerge and evolve throughout Europe, the Americas and other continents.

The contents of these writings make room for the complexity of these issues and still there is generous warmth which counters cynicism. This work can offer young people of today constructive insights into finding their own formulations of discourse for how to embrace the under-standing of a world and cultures in constant transition. Chicana/o experience and perspectives are important to the global context, as well as the global context is important to how we understand the Chicana/o experience. The recent criticisms in our own country of unfair electoral practice, of immigration and gun control laws, of race and hate crimes, of poor health care and an unending list of threats to civil rights, calls for journalism and writing of the caliber of this *calumnista*.

I hope this book is seen as a signal that there is a need to cultivate more journals, magazines and books which contain information and stories of how and what shapes our lives, can lead us to understand how we can actively participate in shaping the events and attitudes needed to build a safe and sustainable future together with others.

Susan Morales Guerra
Oslo, Norway
Originally from San Antonio, Texas

DISCLAIMER— PA' QUE NO CHI...

I was a columnist for the *San Antonio Express-News* for about five years, and I believe I was the first Chicana columnist writing regularly—in my case, monthly for the Op-Ed section—for this paper. I was a "freelance" writer, an independent. I wrote what I wanted and tried to share the conversations my community was having around the kitchen table—in our authentic voice. People used to say I wasn't a *columnista*, Spanish for columnist, I was a *calumnista*, a bilingual word play combining calumny and *columnista*, meaning to my community that I was telling truths that were sometimes so hurtful and scandalous, they seemed like lies.

I am sorry if I hurt anyone with these columns. Just don't believe in wasting ink.

Yes, I have the rights to my *calumnas*. I wrote one column a month for about five years—these are some of my very best. I got paid big bucks, about $150/each, and some of them took two weeks to research and write. And, yes, I really believe in the First Amendment, too. What's the use of "free speech" if you don't use it?

I've also included essays published elsewhere during this decade or so, plus, unpublished work and poetry as well.

If you're wondering, I'm a Tejana, born here, papers and everything. And yes, it's very possible to speak, read and write English and Spanish equally well. And I'm very fluent in Tex-Mex too, the new language of this century. Despite my state's fear of languages. And especially, me. And yes, I've paid a very high price for being me.

Regarding the published columns and essays—they are

published here as they first appeared with some minor edits for syntax and clarity. I did include a couple of columns published before 1995 and after 2005, so your sharp eyes can see my evolving voice. Hopefully, I'm a better writer now.

I have changed the titles of some of the published columns to my original titles that were revised by the *San Antonio Express-News* and a few other publications. Mine are so much better. At the end of this book, I've also included the original published titles in quotation marks.

I hope you will see with this book that our voice matters. I'm only saying what so many are thinking. There is power in our voice, and I am not afraid anymore. #TuVozMatters.

While I think I was the "first" Chicana columnist, at least that called herself a Chicana, I trust I will not be the last. There are better writers out there that you need to read.

And a special message to researchers, librarians, and The Goddess of Tejas History: Because many of these pieces were written during the "Time of Floppy Disks," and I had an agent who protected them from the internet, and I did not keep them organized, it was a nightmare trying to find them again. I spent many, too many, hours and dimes at the microfiche inside the "Enchilada Library" in San Antonio. A few of the published pieces may not correlate exactly with the dates I've listed, and one or two may not be in the right published house. I tried. All you freelancers and independents, pay attention to my mistakes. When there is a question, I have placed an * asterisk so you will know to check if needed. It seems that I typed and listed the date that I wrote many of these pieces, but didn't record when precisely they were published, and where—brilliant.

¡Adelante, anyway! *¡Y dale shine!*

Bárbara Renaud González

DEDICATION TO THE INNOCENT AND THE ONE WHO IS GUILTY

I dedicate this book to my Op-Ed Editor, Linda Vaughan, who trusted, shaped, challenged, and framed my voice when I was writing monthly columns for the *San Antonio Express-News*. To the late Carlos Guerra, fellow *peleonero* and regular columnist, who helped me understand the *alma* in the Alamo. RIP, Carlos. And happy fishing.

And to Mrs. Galloway. For teaching me to read. First grade, Olton, Texas. You understood that I peed in my *chones* 'cause I didn't know how to speak English.

And the guilty innocent: I especially thank our former Governor and President, George W. Bush, who gave me the righteous rage that got me to Santiago de Chile, and who proved he has no clue what it is to be born in Tejas.

Las Nalgas de JLo

JLo's Booty

I am a writer...I belong to the people who have
given me language. Rubén Darío once wrote:
"Con los pobres del mundo quiero echar mi suerte."
I am a son of that despised piece of ground we call the border.
My fate lies with the people who gave me breath.
—Benjamin Alire Sáenz, from *Elegies in Blue,* 2002

You know what the Alamo is?
A monument to a war that we won but really lost.
—Sandra Cisneros

I.

THEY SAY I'M NO LADY

HAVE YOU SEEN PEACH?

I'm from Peach, the brown
man in the wheelchair says.
Durazno in Spanish. Succulent,
ice cream made at home, peach
cobbler and southern brandy—
the best medicine, roasted calabasa,
pumpkin from the wood-burning stove
and brown sugar. He grew up
with café con leche in the mornings, gone
now. All this happened right here, under
the Hemisfair Tower, where he was born
on Peach Street, la calle Peach, aquí
en San Anto.

I was born right here, but everything
is gone, so how did it happen?
Is the Tower my house now?

Have you seen Peach?

AY, HENRY

San Antonio Express-News • Oct 23,1994

Ok, I confess. I was in love with Henry Cisneros once. But I know better now. He is not the man for me. And I am too good for him.

Let me explain.

Like any intelligent Latina, I have made it my business to keep abreast of the latest *chisme* in Henry's complicated life. This is the stuff of novels, but it would make a better *telenovela*. The Greeks have nothing on the Mexicans; that's why my friends say we are God's own fiction—we write the truth and it only seems like magic to everyone else.

It seems like the Hollywoodesque Henry, our mythical champion, will be destroyed by love. I don't know whether to get down on my knees and pray for forgiveness, or curse the furies that brought us this gift of fire to begin with.

Because this is what we all fear. Love. But that's what happened, isn't it?

I don't think he planned to get involved with a married woman—worse, a bleached *gringa*—enough to create a scandal that would cool his political light and scorch his marriage.

If he wanted an affair, I personally know a legion of dedicated *la causa* lawyers, a dozen journalists, some *doctoras chulísimas* and even a *simpática* judge, who believe him to be the best thing since Julio Iglesias met Rubén Blades, but he didn't want them. No. He wanted Linda Medlar, from Lubbock, Texas.

A *machista* wit I know says that Henry's problem is that he doesn't understand the rules. A marriage is a marriage, he says—an affair is an affair... When it's over, the *movida* has to go. You have to have standards, he says.

But Henry didn't choose, did he? Fate chose Henry. And when presented with the choice of a Cabinet appointment, a fresh start at your political career—or a dubious, if glamorous, speechifying future with your lover, what would you do? There are no easy choices between work and love. We wish to have them both. Henry obviously can't.

I, for one, believe that Henry's sense of financial obligation is honorable, but tragic. He is obviously a *macho* man in the truest sense—a man who keeps his word, who takes care of the people he loves.

While I have largely admired his political success, I am dismayed by his choice in women. In a time of *la* Madonna and our motorcyclist governor, Ann Richards, we have seen what an independent woman can be. Yet Henry is surrounded by women whose lives are still defined by him. Mary Alice, his wife, saw her fame ascend alongside his in San Antonio; his lover, Linda Medlar, suffered from his political descent. The wife has forgiven him. His lover has not. But it is not about them.

It is always about Henry.

And this is the way the story goes. If the man is powerful, the woman must be beautiful, and blonde is best. If the woman is successful, the man must be twice as much. We have our standards. After a while, the heart has nothing to do with it. We value ourselves by the love we keep—through marriage papers, money, mayhem, or even murder.

Henry is, and always will be, a legend to most of us. But his story proves that all our worship is never enough. We have made heroes of men who do not trust the worth of their lives without the subservience of women. It is not love that is to blame, but what we have made of it.

Love hurts. And the game of politics is not the game of

love, or is it? Henry has discovered that the women he loves, like any political chip he holds dear—have a price. In his case, it has now come due. Just like politics.

I would have loved him for free.

BROWN MEN CAN'T RUN

San Antonio Express-News • *Oct–Nov 1997*

Don't tell anyone, but Latinos can't play football. It's true, I've seen this for years, starting with high school when I watched our football stars get *apachurrados* by everybody else in the world. Mashed like *frijoles* for supper. Since I went to high schools all over Texas, I got to see Latinos play in a variety of districts from north to south, from Anglo-dominant to Latino-majority schools and where everyone is mixed together. That is why I can say this: Brown men can't run.

So I think we have to find something better to do. Latinos haven't won a state championship in football since Donna High School's win in 1961. There are no Latinos on the University of Texas Longhorn team, so it's not like they could do worse.

Yes, on the pro circuit, we have had Anthony Muñoz, Tony Casillas, Jim Plunkett as the Heisman Trophy winner, and the perennial Mexican kickers like Rafael Septién, Efrén Herrera and Danny Villanueva. Still, not enough. Give it up, *raza.*

Look, football is a waste of time. "We need to be realistic," says Victor Castillo, a former quarterback. "We don't have the innate skills to play football." He speaks from experience. Castillo is the quarterback who passed for 256 yards (it was a slow day) to a certain Warren McVea to win the high school championship for the Brackenridge Eagles of San Antonio in 1962. He went on to college with a football scholarship and came home to coach. McVea also went to college and had a spectacular career as a professional with the Kansas City Chiefs.

"We're not fast enough," says the 5-foot-10-inch Castillo, now back at his alma mater as an assistant principal. But football is a good thing, he asserts. If you're exceptional, the opportunities are there, he believes.

Castillo goes on to give me the old football-is-the-game-of-life-so-we-need-to-play-it-no-matter-what theory. I don't buy it anymore. I think we Latinos know what life is about. We know how tough life is. If anyone knows what it is to be trampled, tackled, kicked around, booed and humiliated, it is us. To get up despite it all. And we don't need football to teach us that lesson.

Look, football has become an expensive game, from the investment at the high school level, to the price of the tickets to see a Cowboys game. All the way to a city's taxes for a shiny new arena.

Consider the high schools that won state championships last year and in the recent past: Austin Westlake, Lewisville, Grapevine, Odessa-Permian, Highland Park, Dallas Carter. None of these schools are poor. Schools like Brackenridge that are now mostly Latino don't have the resources, the facilities, the coaches, the contacts, to create a winner. That's why a football team isn't worth the financial and emotional hassle.

I know that there are men who don't agree with me. "We don't have a level playing field," says a football fanatic. "Our boys are getting bigger all the time. But our schools can't compete. We don't go to the right colleges. The scholarships out there are limited. The coaches won't take chances on us. We are overlooked and there is no institutional pipeline for our high school athletes." He takes a breath. "Our biggest obstacle is that we are conditioned to believe we can't make it in the pros."

Puras petunias. Sure, that's why Latinos are all over the

World Series in baseball and soccer's World Cup. And that's why we have so many *macho* men in boxing and marathons. Football is an All-American thing, and we think we have to play to prove ourselves. To belong. *Por favor.* While we're messing around with Friday nights, the *gringos* are going to take over professional soccer—if they haven't already. And then what? Really, is it too much to ask that one of the Texas Rangers hitting a baseball be a Tejano?

And don't tell me to wait. We need professional athletes today, not *mañana.* I think what really matters is that we find a way to seduce our young men and women into sports—with the attention and money and jackets and pep rallies—and cheerleaders—that we give to football—where they can win big.

"But we have the *corazón*," says the football freak. And I do. That is why I'm tired of imitating others. Life is a brutal game, and we're already way behind.

The last thing we need is to be carrying a football, too.

THE ULTIMATE TACO DIET

San Antonio Express-News • *July 25, 1998*

You know it's ready when the grease is sliding down your arm.

My friend Tita still rhapsodizes over the *tamales* she had at her brother's wedding last year. *Barbacoa, enchiladas, arroz, frijoles refritos* (with real bacon bits), flour *tortillas, chicharrones, tripitas, tostadas, sopapillas… Ay,* she licks her fingers in the total and complete ecstasy of Crisco.

"*Ven a comer.* This food is how I show you my love," my mother tells me when she concocts my favorite dishes, like the shrimp soup that we share when my brother is dying. We eat to celebrate because we have survived, Antonia the historian tells me. It's a working-class food, she reminds me. Like jazz, our food has become a universal cuisine made from the very margins of existence.

"So why are we so *gorditos*," I ask her? Seriously, when is the last time you saw a skinny adult—no, not how you looked *en tus tiempos* twenty years ago when everyone was after you. It's shocking how our exquisite teenagers and children are swollen with flesh instead of muscle. And don't give me the genetics business either, because Latinos on the other side of the border don't have the puffy *taco* look—just go visit the interior of the country and look around—though they're happily on the road to cholesterol-nation too.

Look, people don't come to San Antonio to see the River-walk. They come to eat, because we make the kind of *fajitas* and *margaritas* that make you forget what your problem is with people like us. We are one of the poorest cities in the country, and also the fattest. Maybe the two are connected?

Salsaronic, nachoricious, muy delicious. If you think Tex-Mex is good, the original was to die for, and they did. Just ask Rolando Briseño, a visual artist who paints table settings about food as nature, food as sexuality, food as consumption, and food as conquest. Despite the North American perception of Mexican fast food as a narrow collection of *tacos* and *burritos*, Mexican cuisine contains over a thousand dishes surpassed only by the Chinese, notes Amalia Mesa-Baines in her introduction to Briseño's work at the Instituto Cultural Mexicano. I guess they never tried the *jalapeño* gravy at Church's. The *burrito último,* or the monster *taco*.

Yo quiero saber why our diet is killing us? It's not like we don't know how to eat. Yellow, blue, purple, black, speckled, our maize existed in dozens of flavors when the Spanish arrived. By that time, the indigenous peoples had perfected two hundred varieties of the *tamal*, and the children's cornmeal drink we know as *atole* was flavored with blends of herbs, *chile* and honey. Devoted to their gardens, our ancestors preferred the bluegreen plants, which symbolized the union of water and vegetation. They stewed them, made them into *salsas*, soups, and ate them raw. We traded all this for baloney sandwiches?

When I was growing up, my mother never had Cokes in the house because we couldn't afford it. Cookies and chips were a rare treat. Now they're always in the cupboard. My mother is proud to be able to buy these foods, no, convinced that they are essential to the good life. I was raised in the country with the fresh vegetables that most young people today have never tasted, just ask them. One time my mother boiled *quelite* while my father teased her mercilessly for bringing home a royal green weed that she and I cut down all summer in the fields. His idea of vegetables, a World

War II veteran, was a clinical slab of lettuce, a tomato wafer, maybe a chip of cucumber (if he was feeling adventurous), and a cup of Thousand Island dressing. The other day I read that *quelite* is a kind of wild spinach.

Somehow, I think the absolute diet is the one that begins with knowing who we are. The diet I am searching for, I guess, is about loving myself enough to eat as if I mattered to the world. It means that I respect my ancestors every time I put a fork in my mouth. It means that my table is a creation of all the recipes at my disposal. And all that I am. It's not an easy diet, and it never ends, because this isn't one you'll find in a how-to book.

I am always hungry, but it's a hunger for something that has no name. It tastes like those fried black beans I had in Guatemala during the civil war, prepared by the indigenous women who the soldiers hawk-watched as they fiddled with their machine guns to warn us. Savoring those *frijoles negros* was like a chocolate breeze, a palmful of caviar, the flametip of cognac all at once.

That's when I understood. That's when my diet began.

Class
perspective } part
resources   of our
               diet?

CERVEZA-TIME!

San Antonio Express-News • *Sep 10, 1995*

I need a drink.

This month, we sold our heritage once again for the price of a beer.

In their shiniest campaign yet, the Coors Brewing Co. has unleashed a unique promotion in Texas and California around *Diez y Seis de Septiembre*, Hispanic Heritage Month and National Literacy Month.

In a "Fight for Literacy" with boxing champ Julio César Chávez as the spokesman, Coors has emblazoned the commemorative cans with Julio's champion belt, his gloves and his signature. César Chávez must be turning in his grave.

"Latinos have an alarming 54 percent illiteracy rate," the company says in its press packet. And the silver bullets include a toll-free hotline for literacy information, in small print and readable if you're sober.

"Julio César Chávez is a strong role model for Hispanics," Coors spokeswoman Melissa McCann intones. "His point is that you can do a lot on your own. It doesn't take a formal education." That's true. The last book that Julio César probably opened was his checkbook.

If it doesn't take a formal education, then why is Coors promoting literacy? Because they want us drunk and stupid. For years, according to a report issued by the Center for Science in the Public Interest, titled "Marketing Disease to Hispanics," alcohol and tobacco companies have targeted Latinos with major marketing campaigns.

"They are quick to spot an opportunity. They know how to sell products," says Ed Fitch, a marketing editor at Advertising Age, in the report. And they have discovered our weakness—*la familia*—and the family of our family—our culture.

As Latinos, our heritage is rich with tradition. Yet, all we are celebrating is our very destruction if we allow Coors and other companies to exploit our most sacred days. Celebrate, the ads say. And cry later, *pendejos*, they mean.

According to the Texas Commission on Alcohol and Drug Abuse, Latinos, who make up about 25% of the population in Texas, were a disproportionate 38% of DWI, or Driving While Intoxicated, arrests in Texas.

California is worse, with Latinos accounting for 45% of all adult arrests for DWI, where they are 36% of the population. Ray Chavira, a member of the Los Angeles Commission on Alcoholism, says that "we have been bamboozled. We should be staggering to the ballot box instead of the jailhouse."

But don't count on our Latino leaders to bail us out. Lisa Navarette with the National Council of La Raza, NCLR, one of the most prominent Latino organizations in the nation, says that "NCLR is very impressed with Coors' commitment to eradicating illiteracy... Whatever they do with marketing is up to Coors." Their recent $100,000 gift from the beer company has not muted the feisty organization, she says.

Belén Robles, president of the League of United Latin American Citizens, or LULAC, was unaware of the promotion, and initially stated that "any type of literacy is a good idea," then reconsidered. She had a "bit of a problem" with the specific promotion of literacy on a beer can.

"They give to pity what they owe to justice," asserts Chavira, quoting from the French writer Victor Hugo. And Coors has said it wants to help us learn to read.

In its pity, it has donated $5.2 million to literacy projects in the last five years. Its contributions to scores of Latino organizations would impress even Pancho Villa. Coors contributes to LULAC's national, state and regional conventions, to the American G.I. Forum, and the Mexican American Legal Defense and Educational Fund (MALDEF). Coors also sponsored singer Tish Hinojosa's appearance at the National Association of Hispanic Journalists' meeting in El Paso, Texas.

"I don't think the contribution means we have been silenced," says Gilbert Bailón, the advocate-minded president for the journalists. "Some have questioned whether we should be taking money from beer companies." He didn't think that Latino journalists were compromised in any way, even if the stories weren't being written.

Maybe we can't read, but we know a good *cerveza* when we see one. Latino demographics account for an increasing market share for all beer companies and our relative youth means that there will be loyal beer drinkers for years to come. And Coors is doing something right, sloshing to third place in the Latino market. In 1994, it had net sales of $1.66 billion, up 5.2% from the year before. The company recorded a net income, a profit of $58.1 million in that same year. There goes our justice.

Coors, remembered for its arch-conservative stances in the past, would agree that virtue pays. The real reward of virtue is to have little to apologize for, or to repent, at the end of your life, goes the American work ethic. Wealth is to be valued, explains Christopher Lasch, but chiefly because it serves as one of the necessary preconditions of moral and intellectual cultivation. In other words, money should be valued so that we can reach our potential. In 1993, Latinos had the distinction of significantly contributing to the 9,672 deaths that were involved with alcohol in Texas. But Coors says that it is not responsible. They're right. We are all to blame.

The priest Miguel Hidalgo, who died fighting for all those *mestizos* like us who had no wealth and made others even richer, was a virtuous man too. On September 16, 1810, with one glorious *grito*, the war for Mexican Independence began.

And still we are not free.

MEJOR PUTO QUE JOTO

San Antonio Express-News • Sep 10, 2000

Many years ago from the top of a ferris wheel, I watched my
teenage classmates chasing someone like a dog that smells
a rabbit. Then I saw a blur of a boy, running and looping
around the carnival rides, strangely familiar in the way his
jeans fit him, his graceful hips escaping the pack of boys
who followed him.

Why, I asked my boyfriend, as we watched suspended
above the riot below, were they chasing him?

He's not like the rest of us, he answered. Now he's gonna
get it.

Homosexual. Gay. Lesbian. Those are the nice words we
call them because we're for diversity and tolerance of others.
But we're still chasing them, only now we do it with our
passivity and silence in the face of hateful laws and those
who use pens to shoot them down.

If you're gay, you can't be in the Boy Scouts. Or the
military. Unless you want to lie. Don't ask. Don't tell.

If he's a teacher, don't tell the parents. If she's a lawyer,
don't offend the judge. They can't get married. It seems
like the only institution that protects them is the Catholic
Church—the place that protests way too much, if you know
what I mean.

I believe that gay rights are the civil rights of this
century. Does that offend you? Did it offend you when
African-Americans weren't allowed to swim in the public
pool? Or when people like me couldn't speak Spanish in
school? Or when women couldn't have a career? Then go
back—to the past. Some of the most hateful and degrading
remarks I have heard about gays and lesbians are from those

who demand their Black/Brown/feminist rights the most. How soon we forget.

Who has contributed more to society, Magic Johnson, who slept with thousands of women, or James Baldwin, a writer and civil rights thinker who was shunned by the movement because he was gay?

Socrates, who is credited with so much of our democratic tradition, wrote that erotic passion, such as the one he had for a younger man, was a divine madness, one that was connected to the passions of poetry and philosophy. Know thyself, he said. Knowledge of one's true life leads one to a virtuous life.

Michaelangelo painted the Sistine Chapel to honor the duality of God. Tchaikovsky composed the romantic ballet of *Swan Lake*. Rock Hudson was a secret until the end, but the androgyny of Marlene Dietrich, with her suits and top hat, made her famous throughout the world.

Then there was *A Passage to India* written by E. M. Forster, and jazz artist Bessie Smith, women's rights pioneer Susan B. Anthony, and the most American of poets, Walt Whitman—all who pursued homosexual or bisexual relationships whether they were married or not.

Should we erase these people from history? Burn their art? Their books, their inventions? Do we tell them that we forgive them as long as they deny their being? The passion, according to Socrates, that is the same as their art?

Shall we, in this century, prevent them from getting married, from becoming a policeman, a Boy Scout, a politician, or stop them from saving our soul? Because they are doing it already, I promise you.

Perhaps homosexuality, in the hands of someone such as Leonardo Da Vinci and his *Mona Lisa*, is a gift that is as mysterious as her smile. If a dahlia can bloom on a cactus, *acoctili*, as the Aztecs call them, and there are butterfly wings that are a sexual mosaic of male and female, isn't it possible that our sexuality is just as unique and necessary to the cycle of life?

Isn't it possible that the Pope is wrong on this one? He's been wrong before. Or shall we wait for the apology that's sure to come in the next century?

As for me, please tell that young boy or that young girl being chased right now by a pack of altar boys, that I'm sorry I didn't stop them at the ferris wheel.

Next time, I will defend you. Like I wish someone had defended me.

The Ashes of Lent

San Antonio Express-News • Mar 1999

Raquel gave up candy for Lent. She goes to mass every Sunday with her family, and is trying to lose weight for her new Easter dress. Mercedes has given up soft drinks, Salvador—his favorite six-pack, and Jesse has given up chasing women—but not catching them.

He died for our sins, and so we give up watching our favorite soap opera. It is so hard to sacrifice. That's why we have martyrs and saints. They were the kind of people who walked around barefoot, never tasted pizza, defended the poor, took care of the sick like Mother Teresa. Some were even killed for their belief in a God who said that slaves were the same as a king. As I understand it, one such prophet named Jesus raised such a commotion that he was ultimately, well, you know the ending to this story. Which is like a beginning too.

For a man who hung out with lepers, cripples, and a prostitute named María Magdalena, Jesus has moved up in the world. He's now real close and personal with senators and governors who are compassionate and conservative—something like having sex and keeping your virginity too. Jesus, a single man who never married or had children, is now the symbol for tradition, like the family which includes a man, woman and their two children. He never held down a real job, but he has confirmed fortunes for people who are *la crème brûlée de la cream*—famous, successful, because they pray to him.

Jesus didn't die, how can I put this, for school vouchers as an answer to unequal public schools, he wanted to create another society. He was a radical, *de punta a pie*, who

believed that everyone was equal. He called for people to
serve one another, not to rule over others. If this is true, it
seems to me that he would be on the side of the peasants of
Chiapas, the indigenous people who were massacred by the
government of Guatemala, the children who have televi-
sions but no books in the projects of San Antonio.

It took some centuries, but the name of Jesus, after a few
wars, grew to be interpreted by different groups in different
ways. There were Catholics and some Protestants who called
themselves Puritans who arrived illegally to a new land.
In his name, the Native peoples of North America almost
vanished. In his name, the peoples of Mesoamerica were
enslaved. You see, the Indians didn't believe in Jesus, and
therefore deserved their fate. By this time, the cult of Jesus
included the rich who took pity on the poor and gave to
the Church because they felt guilty, but still wanted to get
to heaven. Then there were the masses of poor who gave
up resisting from the midst of their living hell, hoping for
a heaven that had been promised them because they had
suffered so much. In this way, greed and humility in his
name meshed to become the kind of oppressive society that
Jesus died for.

Jesus was perfect because we are taught that he was the
son of God who walked with us. This is not a man who
had a weight problem, or went to therapy, because he *was*
therapy.

If he were here today, I doubt that he would be addicted
to praline ice cream, cigars, surfing the internet or Chilean *empanadas.* He probably wouldn't spend weekends
watching football, either. If he were here today, he—or
she—wouldn't live very long before getting shot or going to
jail. That's what happens to people who raise holy *infierno*
all over the world.

The trouble is that we forget that his perfection rested
in his serving others. Somehow we confused his lessons
with serving ourselves to prove to him how worthy we are.
A bigger house in the suburbs, more land and trees to tear
down, a Sony for the bedroom, a diamond necklace for the
quinceañera, we work hard to show the Man how special I
am.

In our quest for perfection, we have missed the *we*
suffering, caused by the glorious in *me*. A minimum wage
that isn't. Welfare that keeps children away from their
mothers. The innocent racism spinning its morals while we
drop out, go to prison, and create the kind of men who kill a
policeman because they're desperate. We want fast-food and
a slow death. While the earth gasps with pollution.

The story of Jesus has been told badly, another chapter
to read for history class before the test. Too bad, because
its essence is that when we serve others, we become a more
perfect self, and find the divine in ourselves. Our purpose in
life. And that isn't something you can buy, even if you spend
your whole life searching for it at the malls. Or at the clubs.
Or at church.

I think Jesus scared people so much that he is now the
kind of king that he rebelled against. Jesus would have been
a Zapatista, I'm sure. Not Vicente Fox. Not Ricky Martin.
Not even President Bush, who talks about him constantly.

Jesus, help me not be afraid to be like you.

When Love is the Color Blue/ The Police

[handwritten: lack accountability juxtaposition]

Previously Unpublished • Aug 3, 2004

Carmen never thought she would fall in love with a cop.

And never dreamed she would be the one arrested when he began hurting her.

Up until then, this lovely college-educated woman didn't want a man like her father: You know the type, *comadre. Mexicano* and bad-*macho*. Ugly-*macho*. The kind of man who beat up her mother when he was drinking. *Borracho-macho*.

But we women fall in love with men like our fathers, don't we? And suffer the consequences. But this is really a story about how the police—who are the ones guarding us—are the ones we should guard ourselves from, as well.

I can prove it. Amnesty International has ranked San Antonio the second-highest city in the nation for police misconduct. Police misconduct means excessive force. False arrest. Malicious prosecution. If you still don't understand, just ask most young Brown men in downtown San Antonio and they'll explain it to you. In my years of working with teenagers and college-age students, I've heard too many stories of how often they've been pushed, shoved and cussed out by a violent or prejudiced cop.

[handwritten: racial problem culture it you want better]

Blue, it seems, is the color of hate.

Or it's the color of love spoiled by an apple hurled at a woman's body—like in the recent story of the television reporter Gina Galaviz and former policeman, and now Councilman, Ron Segovia's very public denouement.

***

In the early eighties, former City Councilwoman María Antonietta Berriozábal wanted a Civilian Review Board that would have the power to challenge the police's authority. She didn't get it. San Antonio has a chicken-and-wolf kind of system where the real power remains under the police and Chief Ortiz. So that we, the citizens of San Antonio, can't independently investigate or discipline the police.

Most critically, we can't subpoena the police in controversial cases.

In other words, if you have a complaint against the police, pray hard. Because a woman like Gina Galaviz and Carmen (not her real name because she's so afraid) have the courts, the District Attorney's office, and the media—unless it's one of their own—insulating their colleagues and too often, glorifying the cops.

It may not matter to you now, but it will if you ever confront the police. Or if they confront you.

A democratic society needs the men and women in blue. But not in the shape of bruises on a woman's back, on her slender wrists. I am in love with *machos,* yes, but not the blue that steals the color from the sky and blackens this city.

911.

EL MAYOR, B.C.
(BEFORE CASTRO)

*Undetermined • *2005*

*Better to turn San Antonio upside down to find you a
good husband, than to look for a good mayor.*
—Sandra Cisneros

Mayor. Sounds good, doesn't it? There are five major cities
that could elect a Latino *alcalde* this year. New York, Houston, Miami, Los Angeles, and of course, the city named for
a saint who helps women searching for good husbands. Or
good mayors. If you have faith, that is. In San Antonio.

"Who would want to be mayor of this city?" jokes Dr.
Arturo Vega, political science professor at the University of
Texas San Antonio (UTSA). "We have a weak mayor system...the City Manager runs the city." Water conservation?
Economic development? Inner-city revitalization? Technology? Education? Who wouldn't want all these good things
for the city? he questions. *El detalle* is whether the candidate
has the skills to make his agenda a reality. He means the
ability to leverage his informal power to coalesce people
around his agenda. Because that's all the power he has.

And comparing the sexiness of former gang-banger
and current state assembly leader (he has removed the
"born to kill" tattoo from his past) of Antonio Villaraigosa's
mayoral potential in Los Angeles to San Antonio's wannabe
Ed Garza, is like comparing the grandness of the Pacific
Ocean to—well—Padre Island. Big difference, says Dr. Josie
Méndez-Negrete, a California native and UTSA sociologist.
The mayor of Los Angeles has institutional power, she says.
And it's significant, Dr. Vega underscores, that Villaraigosa

is returning to his hometown after a stint of legislative experience.

"If Ed Garza won't even return phone calls to María Antonietta Berriozábal" (former mayoral candidate in 1991 who forced Judge Nelson Wolff into a runoff), says Dr. Vega, and a sentiment echoed by other Latino activists I spoke to, "then he is either naive about coalitions—or he is running from his ethnicity." In contrast, Henry Cisneros was *"el hijo del pueblo,"* another activist tells me. As a son of the people, he spoke Spanish, and energized the southside and westside to vote for him (1981-1989). Unfortunately, President George W. Bush speaks more Spanish than Ed Garza—whatever that means. And it was the conservative Bannwolf who pretended to lead the César Chávez March this year.

Not that ethnicity—or gender—matters that much in politics. They make a difference, explains Professor Vega. But not always. There is a norming process in politics. Like the influence of PAC money and interest groups. State Senator Gonzalo Barrientos, and former Chairman of the Hispanic Caucus in the state legislature, told me years ago that he dared not challenge then-Governor George W. Bush's popularity. He wanted a committee chairmanship first. "Bigger fish to fry," retorts Professor Vega. Mr. García goes to Washington. The irony, he says, is that our politicians go into office to reform the system, but they end up supporting the system instead. Think PGA Golf Course and the water that it will require to keep the grass green. Water for the 1000-room Marriott. Water for all those microchips that Bannwolf needs for his biotechnology dreams. But who has the power to challenge the developers?

Not the mayor. It will depend on the quality of the coalitions he can muster. "There are many short-sighted development strategies," says Dr. Vega, "that will have long-term development costs."

"Syphilis and gonorrhea," shrugs an activist, quoting Eldridge Cleaver. That's the real difference between Garza and Bannwolf. Leadership? Forget it, says Dr. Méndez-Negrete. "We're buying into the notion of established positions of power and authority." That doesn't make a real leader, she emphasizes. That kind of representational power "has nothing to do with change."

Former Councilwoman Berriozábal remembers Ed Garza's *abuelito*, who owned a car garage on the Westside that is now deteriorated. How hard he worked, she muses. What good people they were. She doesn't say it, but I imagine that she's thinking about how the A&M land planner has abandoned the little garage that was fundamental to his college degree.

A Latino mayor in San Antonio after the time of Henry Cisneros? "If it doesn't happen now, it may not happen for a long time," worries Rosie Castro, a long-time activist and mother of Julián Castro, whose Harvard-educated son is running for City Council in District 7. Despite the *mestizo* moments of the tourist hype, Latinos in this city don't run City Public Service, San Antonio Water System, the banks, or the County Judge's office, she points out. Zero. *Nada.*

"It would be nice for my children to see a Latino mayor," says Professor Vega. "Even if he is just a symbol."

As long as we understand that's all he is.

San Antonio, *por favor,* I beg you, one day soon bring us a real mayor. We've waited so long.

Sunday, January 14, 2001

Texas must learn lesson from escape

They are armed and dangerous. Those seven men who escaped from the Connally prison in Kenedy are murderers, robbers, kidnappers, rapists. They are not nice people. They most likely killed a police officer. A bloodbath — if they are captured — is inevitable. But . . .

There is a part of me that wants them to make it . . . if we don't learn anything from all of this.

Barbara Renaud Gonzalez

Texas leads the nation imprisoning its citizens. The Bureau of Justice Statistics reports that at the end of 1999, there were 706,600 Texans in prison, jail, parole or probation on any given day. In a national context, nearly one in five new inmates was added to the nation's prisons was in Texas.

I don't know about you, but I doubt whether the great state of Texas knows how to manage so many bad people.

And our crime rate is still 11 percent above the national average. Throughout the prison-building frenzy of the 1990s, Texas added five times as many prisoners as New York. Yet, the Lone Star State's crime figures are much less impressive than those damn Yankees — *their* crime rate dropped twice as much as ours. The two are compared because the state populations are relatively matched.

It's no secret that more than half of the men in prison are being held for non-violent crimes. Or that 21 percent of the prison population is in there for drug-related charges. 45 percent of the prison population has a history of drug or alcohol abuse. Very few of them have fathers they remember — or who visit them in prison. The average education is ninth grade, and while more education is possible in prison, it is not required.

While one of every 20 Texas adults is under some form of criminal justice control, one out of three young black men is in prison, jail, probation, or on parole. There are no specific numbers for Latinos, but when I've visited the prisons, they are overwhelmingly black and brown.

On the way to Beeville for Christmas, which is 30 miles from Kenedy, the busdriver asked me if I was a prison guard. You see, my former hometown, once boasting Chase Naval Field, is now a prison town — a place with not one but two prisons, the Garza and the McConnell units that now hold thousands of men.

It is a town, says my friend Victor, where the prisoners are "cleaning the cemeteries, (fixing) the bridges, putting up Christmas lights at the courthouse." They are taking civilian jobs, he charges. Victor resents the way that the city fathers have allowed the town

to become a prison at the expense of its citizens. Anyway, he says, there is not such a big difference between those inside and outside, explaining that he has partied with prison guards.

"There are more drugs in there than out here," says Victor. "One toke out here costs $2," he explains. "But in there it costs $10." And guess who is tempted to act as the middleman? The guards. Their salaries are low, he says. "About $1200 a month to start."

My sister, who, shall we say, knows something about the underworld, expands on this point. "If the guards go in there thinking that the (inmates) are dumb, they're in for a surprise," she laughs. "Just because they don't have high school degrees doesn't mean that they aren't . . . they are street-smart."

And the prison guards? "People who want to have power over somebody worse off than them."

Or just people who want to stay in Beeville, says Victor. And there are no other jobs.

Ultimately, my sister says, the prisoners and the guards are separated by a very thin line of "what ifs — but for the grace of God go I," and many recognize it. The smartest inmates have figured out that they are in a prison that is just inside another prison and then another, because it's all about "fear and intimidation," she says. "Only the guards get paid for it."

"Twenty-four hours a day, seven days a week, and the prisoners have time to think," she says. About how society put them in there. About the power of the few to imprison the many.

About revenge.

That's right. If you're poor, black or Latino in this state, our racist history seasoned with our hang-em-high frontier, laced with an eye-for-an-eye Christianity have created a lethal stew of punishment and cruelty.

That's why there will be more tragic deaths. Of policemen. Prison guards.

More assaults. Victims. And more escapes. Lots of blood.

But that's the way we like it in Texas. Armed and dangerous.

Barbara Renaud Gonzalez is a free-lance writer in San Antonio.

ARMED AND DANGEROUS

San Antonio Express-News • Jan 14, 2001

They are armed and dangerous.

Those seven men who escaped from the Connally prison in Kenedy, Texas, last December 13th are murderers, robbers, kidnappers, rapists. They are not nice people. They most likely killed a police officer. A bloodbath—if they are captured—is inevitable. But...

There is a part of me that wants them to make it...if we don't learn anything from all of this.

Texas leads the nation in imprisoning its citizens. The Bureau of Justice Statistics reports that at the end of 1999, there were 706,600 Texans in prison, jail, on parole, or probation on any given day. In a national context, nearly one in five new prisoners added to the nation's prisons were in Texas.

I don't know about you, but I doubt whether the great state of Texas knows how to manage so many bad people.

And our crime rate is still 11% above the national average. Throughout the prison-building frenzy of the 1990s, Texas added five times as many prisoners as New York. Yet, the Lone Star state's crime figures are much less impressive than those damn Yankees—their crime rate dropped twice as much as ours. The two are compared because the state populations are relatively matched.

It's no secret that over half of the men in prison are being held for non-violent crimes. Or that 21% of the prison population is in there for drug-related charges. 85% of the prison population has a history of drug or alcohol abuse. Very few of them have fathers they remember—or who visit them in prison. The average education is 9th grade, and while more education is possible in prison, it is not required. While one of every 20 Texas adults is under some form of criminal justice control, one out of three young Black men are in prison, jail, on probation, or parole. There are no specific numbers for Latinos, but when I've visited the prisons, they are overwhelmingly Black or Brown.

On the way to Beeville for Christmas, which is thirty miles from Kenedy, the bus driver asks me if I am a prison guard. You see, my former hometown, once boasting Chase Naval Field, is now a prison-town—a place with not one but two prisons, the Garza and the McConnell units which now hold thousands of men.

It is a town, says my friend, Victor, where the prisoners are "cleaning the cemeteries, [fixing] the bridges, putting up Christmas lights at the courthouse." They are taking civilian jobs, he charges. Victor resents the way that the city fathers have allowed the town to become a prison at the expense of its citizens. Anyway, he says, there is not such a big difference between those inside and outside, explaining that he has partied with prison guards.

"There are more drugs in there than out here," says Victor. "One toke" (a marijuana cigarette) out here costs $2, he explains. "But in there it costs $10." And guess who is tempted to act as the middleman? The guards. Their salaries are low, he says, "about $1,200 a month to start."

My sister, Leticia, who, shall we say, knows something about the underworld, expands on this point. "If the guards go in there thinking that the [inmates] are dumb, they're in for a surprise," she laughs. "Just because they don't have high school degrees doesn't mean that they aren't…they are street-smart." And the prison guards? "Bottom of the barrel…people who can't make it anywhere else…people who want to have power over somebody worse off than them."

Or just people who want to stay in Beeville, says Victor. And there are no other jobs.

Ultimately, Leticia says, the prisoners and the guards are separated by a very thin line of what-ifs, but-for-the-grace-of-God-go-I, and many recognize it. The smartest inmates have figured out that they are in a prison that is just inside another prison and then another because it's all about "fear and intimidation," she says. "Only the guards get paid for it."

"Twenty-four hours a day, seven days a week, and the prisoners have time to think," she says. About how society put them in there. About the power of the few to imprison the many.

About revenge.

That's right. If you're poor, Black or Latino in this state, our racist history seasoned with our hang-em-high frontier, laced with an eye-for-an-eye Christianity has created a lethal stew of punishment and cruelty that we will keep despite any logic I can throw at you. Any sympathy I can make you feel.

That's why there will be more tragic deaths. Of policemen. Prison guards. More assaults. Victims. And more escapes. Lots of blood.

But that's the way we like it in Texas. Armed and dangerous.

LOS DROPOUTS

San Antonio Express-News • *May 2000

Ayala. Briseño. Cárdenas. For every proud graduate who walks across that stage to pick up a high school diploma next month, there is a dropout watching from the shadows.

No matter what the schools tell you, the fact is that two out of every five ninth-graders in Texas don't finish high school in four years. We will be lucky this year if less than 150,000 young people drop out across the state. There have been more than 1.2 million dropouts in the last twelve years.

Díaz. Elizondo. Frausto. We can change this scenario. It's so obvious that I never found it in any research about dropouts. Because nobody wants to talk about it.

The answer is to send our children to the poor, inner-city schools.

García. Herrera. In the first place, those schools aren't poor in the way that you think. That's where most of us come from, and we did pretty well, ¿*verdad?* Second, we can now offer our children the best of all possible worlds in ways our own parents could not: extended travel, internships, the luxury of museums, books, the conversations of our educated friends. Instead of what is not important: television and the mall. Or a new car for *mijito*. Third, the inner-city schools will give our children a superb lesson in linguistic diversity, cultural expression, and civic exercises in democracy—like the economics of labor and political organizing. And they will get a course in Living Religion: Compassion 101.

Ibarra. Jiménez. Losoya.

You see, we have reached a place of no return in our

public schools. Our great state of Texas ranks at the very bottom in every conceivable educational category. Latino youth account for one out of every seven young adults in the U.S., yet we are one out of every three dropouts. The experts say the attrition rate is higher than ever. I could cite you statistics and studies all day long, but we know the why, and we know the what. So, when? Now.

Méndez. Negrete. Ozuna.

Why do dropouts drop out? What a question. Why did you graduate? Good parents who sacrificed for you, a significant teacher, a counselor, some food on the table. But most of all, someone cared about you, about me, when we needed it most. No, poverty is not the reason that our young people drop out. But poverty is the cause when every single person in that school is poor.

Those young people in their poverty-stricken schools need us, the middle-class. They need our stability, our leadership, our values, our demands. In a critical mass. No amount of legislation, initiatives, mentoring, corporate sponsorships, scholarships—money—all necessary and commendable, will make a substantial difference unless our children are attending those schools as well.

Because if we don't educate them, we Latinos, our beloved *gente*—is going to impoverish this state with the sheer weight of our uneducated, marginalized, disengaged, and at-risk population. You still think that our booming Latino market is something to brag about? So, you think stupidity is sexy?

Prieto. Quiñones. Rendón.

Before you scream and tell me that you cannot sacrifice your children to the inner-city schools, talk to Luti Vela-Gude. Her oldest son, David, is at Harvard this year. (1530 SAT). A product of the poor inner-city schools for most of his life, he "liked it," and was never attacked (imagine!) by the gangs. Though one time in Spanish class the students rolled weed, and of course, there was lots of sleeping in history class. At Harvard, he says, the students don't sleep because they study all the time. And they don't have a *corazón* for anybody but themselves.

Urrutia. Villarreal.

The tragedy of our time is the vast poverty of the world. No, let me rephrase that. The tragedy is the way that we deny the magnitude of poverty in the world, the way we are oblivious to it. The tragedy is—that in our great love for our children, we have not educated them to face its dire consequences. Because, believe me, they will.

Yduñate.

The paradox is that we work so hard to educate our young to become like the people who exploited us in the first place.

Zapata.

We Latinos, who know so much about racism, are prejudiced too. We are prejudiced against the poor. We want democracy for us—but not for anybody else.

It's time to do what the *gringos* and so many others would not do for us without a fight.

Share. *Sí se puede.*

LOS HERMANOS BRISEÑO

San Antonio Express-News • Mar 19, 2001

They shared a bed as children. Built a city from dirt and the
leftover tiles that Uncle Carlos brought them. While other
boys played with cars, Rolando and Alex Briseño dreamed
of a city that only they could imagine—a city of fountains,
plazas and a cathedral with spires. Alex, the smart one, was
always in charge of the city. Rolando, the baby, was the one
who made it beautiful.

After more than ten years, Alex Briseño will say *adiós* at
the end of March to the job that he worked all his life to attain. He was the first Latino city manager, and the first from
el westside, who speaks Spanish fluently, who is a graduate
of Texas A&M and Trinity University. And who has a brother like Rolando. Because his younger, favorite brother is an
accomplished visual artist who has lived in Europe and New
York City. Who has exhibited in cities around the world.
And who is gay.

Unlike Miami's *cubanos*, San Antonio's Mexican population is from the *campesino* class who left Mexico because
the rich landowners controlled everything. Or from the
Tejanos, who lost their land to the Anglo settlers after the
U.S.-Mexican War. Then there are those who are descendants of the Mexican landowners who saw their *haciendas*
confiscated or burned to the ground, who were devoted
to the Church and betrayed by the tyranny of President
Porfirio Díaz.

Rolando and Alex have all these histories inside them. At
different times, in different places. Like the city.

Herencia con corazón, is the way that Rolando, the slim-
mer GQ version of Alex, describes what he wishes the city

could become. He envisions a city that is walkable, with the kind of mass transit that will make his brother Alex return to live in the inner-city they grew up in. He doesn't want a city built for tourists, but a city for its *gente*. A *ciudad* with great public art, the kind that people will come from all over the country to see: murals and painted sidewalks, fiberglass sculpture, and colored-light fountains. Something besides the Alamo crap. His brother, Alex, shrugs. Alex hasn't been to the Alamo since he and Rolando were kids.

"They are hicks," says Rolando, when I ask him why his brothers, with a physician and a millionaire businessman among them, don't buy his abstract paintings. He complains of the American dream of comfort and real estate that precludes art or books. They see themselves paying thousands of dollars for a work of art, he says. Even his brother Alex, he tells me, who is so proud of him, didn't buy the *Moctezuma's Table* painting that hangs proudly in his office. "It was a trade," he sighs, for helping him with the budget planning he needed for the renovated warehouse that he and his partner, Ángel, bought near downtown.

Alex tells me that Rolando has influenced the way he looks at the urban design of the city. He credits Rolando's influence with the "percent for art" program that is now euphemistically called "design enhancement" to please conservative forces in this city. Alex confesses that he has begun to write poetry. How he envies Rolando's cosmopolitan style and experiences. When did you find out that Rolando was gay? I ask. I just knew, he smiles at his brother.

But they don't talk about it. And while Alex loves his brother, he doesn't admire "in your face" gay and lesbian politics.

Rolando's progressive politics have cost him plenty. He has been blacklisted by important arts patrons, by UTSA even, for confronting the paternalism of "I like you as long as you don't challenge me." Alex understands. He tells me a story of a racist councilman who he dares not mention by name. How "he showed them" at the Corps of Cadets at A&M by becoming the "outstanding freshman" despite the way they ridiculed him on Texas Independence Day.

Alex wants to prove he is good enough. Like his father, who was in LULAC. Rolando wants to be respected for who he is. Like his mother, the once-wealthy *mexicana*. Alex is proud of his Spanish, his work ethic, his compassion. Rolando is proud of his Spanish too, and he reminds me that his mother raised him with classical music and Chopin. Not with *conjunto*.

They tease each other, argue about their childhood dream. What a city that was, they remember.

When they shared a bed. Before the city came between them.

THE SUNTAN CLUB

San Antonio Express-News • *Aug 15, 1999*

Every year about this time my skin gets lighter. It happens in aerobics class between the leg lifts and doggie kicks. I'm looking at my sweaty form in the mirror when I realize that I'm not the only brown one anymore. Don't stand out like a fly in milk. It's *sartén* time. The frying pan that some people call the perfect suntan.

The suntan club is one whose membership doesn't include me, though I'm naturally tanned. These are the people who sit outside during lunch to get some sun even if it's 100 degrees. No, thank you.

These are also the women whose weekends are to lay out by the pool, rotisserieing themselves while they fiddle with straps and potions. Then there are the men who chase golf balls on Saturday morning with the guys so that they can get a ruddy complexion—or at least a promotion. They want to look like they know what to do in the outdoors. But of course they don't.

Well, I know what the sun is about. It's about fine dust that sticks like asbestos to your face and rattlesnakes getting some shade and landing on your feet as you turn over the cucumber plant to pick some juicy ones for the gallon bucket that you've been carrying for half a mile.

It's your summer job, and the sun is waiting for you when you come back from having *taquitos* with the rest of the gang under the shade of the flat-bed trailer truck. The sun is mosquitoes, pollen, and a boss-man who drives by every few hours to check on you.

The sun is your wrinkled father, *chicharroneado* from the relentless work, so proud of his fields of watermelon, maize, soybean, wheat. His hands feed a thousand people. And still there is no money.

The sun is for digging ditches for the next luxury stadium, climbing to the roof to patch a suburban home, laying brick for the new shopping center, planting beds of colorful *teresitas* and *margaritas* for the uptown restaurant.

The sun laughs as the man smooths the cement outside the courthouse, leaving his mark in a place that you can only see if you are waiting for the bus, *Chuy '88 c/s.* The sun watches those who are building the Amistad Dam, like my father did in Del Río after they took the harvest.

The sun is the blanket of the poor, say the Mexicans. The suntan club has decided they want the color brown, but not the people who the sun has lovingly wrapped in it, so they have stolen it and now it belongs to them.

They determine who can be brown and when. For instance, it's ugly to be born brown, but it's a status thing if you are able to return the color of iced-tea from a visit to Cancún. Especially if your hair is streaked with blonde highlights and there are no tan lines.

It's not good to be brown and sleep in the middle of the day so that you can go back to work when the sun cools. That kind of brown is lazy. It's good to work during the hottest hours of the day and miss sitting on your porch to admire the full moon when you can be watching television after working so hard and you get a well-deserved heart attack.

It's ok to faint from a sunstroke after walking ten miles for the March of Dimes, but it's not good to pay a little more in penny taxes so that your city can have more trees and buses.

The suntan club has strange rules: the darker your tan, the richer and smarter you must be. And if you are brown from birth, then the poorer and dumber you surely are. Brown is beautiful, but not on me, unless I marry someone who tans, and then I automatically become less brown. Brown depends. Brown depends on who owns the rainbow.

Round sun, red sun, goes the Mexican song. Like a copper coin. Sun, you are so fair in the way you spread your light. You should teach the rich to be just like you.

MUCHACHITAS

San Antonio Express-News • *Aug 13, 2000*

Pink roses on the push-up bra. Translucent blouse. An *ombligo* that's pierced, the flat stomach spandexed into a purple skirt riding so low that if you miss her belly-button you won't forget the elastic of that leopard-skin thong in the back.

Enjoy it, *muchachos*, because summer's over. Beige and white rule in San Antonio schools. Come Monday, it's uniform time.

And believe it or not, both styles are stupid.

On the street, Selena. Christina Aguilera. *La* Jennifer (before she became JLo). These are the images that surround young girls, the celebrities who influence the way they talk, dress, think. Let's face it, slut is in.

When I was 16, I wore shorts up to there too. What was I thinking?

Of getting a boyfriend, that's what.

I wanted to be pretty, popular, hang a senior's ring around my neck. Wanted romance, love, sex, in that order.

Attention. To get that, I tried my best to look like the women the boys admired on television, at the movies. Or the cheerleaders. Not the teachers.

You see, whether it's a jersey halter top or a khaki jumper, it's the same thing. It's about someone else's idea of what a girl should wear. Who she should be.

Back in the day, I wore a uniform too—only it was not called that—it was just called *"la moda,"* or being in style. It was not cool to be different. Like the fat girls, the few *machas* who dressed like boys, or the *artistas* who wore vintage.

Don't you think it's ironic how the business of women's

fashion, owned by men, creates clothes so provocative that girls "have to be protected" at the public schools?

I wonder how many books written by women these young girls get to read in class, how the teachers handle the history of feminism? Do they get art classes, dance or music to compensate for the conformity that they are forced into?

After a lifetime of being dressed by others, most of my girlfriends can't imagine what they would wear if given the chance. We hate those Gap colors on our brown skin, the ridiculous black New York look for San Antonio. Unless you have lots of money, you're stuck with T-shirts, dresses that are too tight, clothes that have absolutely no style—because they're in style.

And so you look like everyone else. Just look around. And think like everyone else. But that's the idea, isn't it?

And the young girl? Who is she? If she is like me, it will take her 30 years to understand what all these uniforms have done to heart, brain, and body. For too long, she will believe that she should please men; that's what her clothes are about, after all.

She will waste many years believing that she has to be like everybody else. She will never be satisfied with how she looks, walks, talks, because it is never as good as the uniforms in her head.

No matter that she goes on to become a Harvard-educated pediatrician, like my friend Annie. She doesn't have the right clothes, which means she isn't good enough. Or she has the right clothes, like another friend, Gloria. And nothing else.

She will waste many years defining herself by what men think. Though she will not understand that, because she has never dressed herself. Much, much, later, she will learn to please herself and no one else.

I want to know in this great time of diversity...why do young girls still have to look the same? How far we have come, *¿verdad?*

I want to know what is so liberating about dressing the same.

And then I want to know why you don't believe how beautiful you really are.

The Car Gods

San Antonio Express-News • *April 9, 2000*

At least there is one commandment I haven't broken. And that is the worship of cars, the real gods of our time. For every two children arriving in this world, a car is born. Guess which one is more expensive. A car is the ultimate graduation present. Not books, not a summer of travel to know the ancestral roots. And if the young man is too poor to get one, he will blow off college for a job to buy one.

A car defines us. A car is manhood. A car is a symbol of power, of status. We call this a ride to freedom. That's right. With little or no public transportation, we aren't free not to have a car.

What would the U.S. be without the automobile? Thanks to Henry Ford and Harvey Firestone's *compadrazgo*, the whole world wants to be like us. Even if our dream-mobile kills and wounds more Americans than all the soldiers who died or suffered in Vietnam. More than guns or smoking, drugs or AIDS.

There are 10 million car-related injuries worldwide and 250,000 deaths on the roads every year. Think of the number of people who died at Hiroshima and Nagasaki—and that was to end the war. Here, the cars won.

Stick around long enough and the weather will change, we say in Texas. Now it's happening all over the world. Why? Our cars need gasoline which pollutes from the fields of production to the stations of consumption. The fumes from burning gasoline are the largest artificial source of atmospheric carbon in the world. To make a long story very short, nothing less than the ecology of the planet is at stake.

Deny this if you want. The Big Three can afford television ads, and I can't. So they must be telling the truth.

Just don't drink while you drive. Texas leads the nation in the number of alcohol-related fatalities, and the governor's answer is to lower the legal amount of alcohol in the blood. *Tonto*, he takes away the bottle but leaves the car. This from the man who brought you Desert Storm, and now the veterans of that glorious war are turning up sick. And dying.

Whatever you do, don't sacrifice your cars. Gasoline is too high, you say.

I think it's too cheap.

The typical American devotes more than 1,500 hours a year (30 hours a week, four hours a day, including Sundays) to his or her car. Driving it. Gas. Tires. Parking and searching for it. Tolls. Tickets. Insurance. And the hours of work required to pay for it.

It takes 1,500 hours to go 6,000 miles. Figure it out yourself. That's three and a half miles per hour. You call this progress?

If the car is to prevail, there's one solution: Get rid of the city.

We've already begun that, stringing suburbs like stale popcorn from here to nowhere. One-fifth of the typical city is devoted to car use. To make room for the cars, distances have to increase. People live far from their work, far from school, far from the supermarket—which then requires a second car for all the errands. Cars, yes—but trees have to go. Hit the road, butterflies and birds. The landscape changes or, rather, is degraded, to serve the car. So that it can see at 70 miles per hour.

So sidewalks shrink. But we don't. We get fat and fatter, so we drive to exercise class. A car drove us to our birth, and a car will take us to our grave. We can't walk even if we want to—it isn't safe after dark. If the criminals don't get you, the cops will stop you, if the dogs don't get you first. People feel sorry for you.

I speak from experience.

But *ay*, the crying over a gallon of gasoline that costs less than a gallon of milk and a little more than a gallon of Coca-Cola on sale. Lower the taxes, we scream to our full-of-gas politicians.

But no road tax can begin to compensate for the social costs. The damaged environment, the medical bills, the noise, the crime, the loss of community that our love of cars has caused. We think that the people of India are crazy because they believe that cows are sacred. Here, cars are sacred.

Which takes me back to the First Commandment.

Ok, ok, so there's another one I haven't broken. Just keep me away from that guy who played Moses.

DAN MORALES,
AFFIRMATIVE ACTION BABY

San Antonio Express-News • May 10, 1998

In Texas, affirmative action is a rattlesnake that bites your hand when you thought it was already dead.

Just ask Dan Morales, our attorney general, who has denied the University of Texas' surprising request to appeal the 1996 Hopwood decision, the landmark ruling that prohibited race-based admissions in higher education. Who would've dreamed that the University of Texas at Austin (UT), no bastion of racial progress, will do it with no help from Morales or Governor George W. Bush.

Since Hopwood, both the University of Texas and Texas A&M have seen their minority enrollment slither to endangered status at the graduate, law and medical schools. Because the Black and Brown population comprises 40% of the state, legal experts say that an appeal could rattle Hopwood's decision to the feet of the Supreme Court. Ouch.

I tell you, there is nothing like affirmative action to expose the magic reality of race relations in this state. Morales was elected in his first race for attorney general because Latinos voted the last name. Bush may go to Tejano music festivals and have a Mexican in-law, but neither man has the *huevos rancheros* to imagine a state that is different from the one they came from—a state that thrives on the appearance of diversity, a state that consumes everything about us except who we really are.

Talk about talkin trash. Affirmative action has been very good to Bush and Morales. Our governor was born rich and has a father who had enough connections to help him

on his way, no matter what he says. Morales got the chance
to go to Harvard Law School while *gringos*, like the ones in
Hopwood, were passed over for debts owed and the intangi-
ble value that minority perspectives bring to the classroom.
But this is a state where *macho* is the symbol of the Alamo,
and our leaders have to pretend that they did it on the *chile*
in their guts and the size of their guns.

Like all myths of empire, the cowboy one is fighting its
last stand, but not before it takes the state down with it.
When I was growing up, Latinos were mostly working-class,
and a negligible percentage of the state's population. We
were romanticized or forgotten, because we weren't a force
to be reckoned with. Now, Latinos and Blacks will comprise
over half of the state's population in 2030. And the demographics are so fast and so stunning that most people can
read the numbers over and over again, but it's like wandering naked into a patch of rattlesnakes—we are paralyzed by
the thought of it. Better to deny that it will ever happen.

Better to pretend that life can go on as before.

Well, *corazón*, the party is over. One-third of the school-
children in Texas are Latinos, thirteen percent are Blacks
and the majority go to public schools that deny them the
chance to compete with Anglos when they get ready to go
to college. Perhaps that's the rub, could it be? Keep Latinos
and Blacks from getting a decent education and then they
won't be able to take their place in this state. That's like
grabbin a rattlesnake by the tail. Somehow I don't think that
minorities are willing to return to the pioneer days, thank
you. Except for Dan Morales.

While Bush and his cronies fiddle with lotteries, not-
in-my-backyard taxes, vouchers, tests, and token appoint-
ments, the next generation of minority students fail. It's
just easier to talk about personal responsibility when our

politicians don't have any.

"Racial quotas, set-asides and preferences do not, in my judgment, represent the values and principles which Texas should embrace," says Morales in his defense of Hopwood.

Excuse me, Dan, but what values and principles does Texas stand for? One of the worst public school systems in the country, that's what.

You see, affirmative action isn't about some underserving minorities going to college. It's about honoring a fundamental tenet of democracy—the right to a free public education in this country.

And it isn't free when we will pay for the prisons and poverty of all those who drop out and our best and brightest have *vamoosed* the state, or don't have the education to lead us out of this sorry mess.

Affirmative action is about believing that all children deserve a good education regardless of what their parents do for a living. Affirmative action isn't about merit or quotas or the middle-class taking advantage, which it does. It's about the ideal of equality.

Remember that word? And it's worth fighting for.

My baby brother, Esteban, at work on a doctorate far away from Texas, is angry that our leaders are high-risking the state's potential with their living in the past. Where is their courage, he asks? If we don't educate people like me, there will be a civil rights movement in the next century that will make the '60s look like children playing with stolen matches. And the sky will explode like a thousand coils of fire.

"What do people think," he says, "that the next generation is too stupid to figure it out sooner or later?"

I want the case to go to the Supreme Court.

Let's get it on.

ME AND KOBE
IN THE BACK SEAT

San Antonio Express-News • Oct 7, 2004

When I was eighteen, I met Kobe Bryant.

Well, he was *mexicano* and a lot shorter and *güerito*, and when I met him he wasn't a professional basketball player. He was playing volleyball on a Sunday afternoon.

But, *¡ay!,* he did look like some kind of god slapping the ball into the air. And the way that he seemed to take over the field! A star around men who obeyed his order. *¡Pa'cá, vato! ¡Muévete! ¡Pégale, idiota!*

Then he noticed me, watching. He smiled.

For a whole month, we were the Hollywood couple *de Tortilla Tech*, otherwise known as UT Pan American in Edinburg. Until one night. My Kobe asked me to go with him to the drive-in. Yes, in small towns, we still had them. And yes, it was stupid for me to trust him, but he was much older than me—twenty-two years old, and a senior! Besides, nothing had happened other than dancing, playing basketball, and some kissing.

When I was eighteen, I was innocent. My father had taught me how to punch men out, but he hadn't told me what to do when someone did that to me. I was innocent about sex, but even more innocent about the power that men have against women—because, now I know, they are afraid of us.

I was hungry too—though I didn't know then that I was looking for love. Or something like it. I was lonely, away from home for the first time, still trying out my new woman's skin. Yes, I wanted—but that isn't what men think we

want. That's just the way to get what we want—which is to
be kissed, embraced, romanced. Welcomed for our body—
yes—but for our dreams, too.

And it was this innocence that followed me into the back
seat with Kobe at the drive-in.

I was lucky. Kobe stopped trying to rape me with my
crying and kicking. I only suffered a purple collar of hickies
around my neck, bruise petals on my wrists. The other kind
of injury—shame—is still with me. It was my fault after all.

Men have told me that Kobe didn't do anything wrong.

First, they say, a woman who goes into a man's hotel
room—or the back seat—or an apartment—knows what is
going to happen.

Second, if a woman says no, the guy should ask again in
five minutes. She may change her mind.

Third, did she complain right away? If a woman doesn't
say anything until a day later, then how can you believe
something happened to her?

Even today, when women are far more sexually aware,
they are innocent about rape. I see them drinking too
much in a nightclub, or pursuing a basketball player who is
swollen with power and stupid-innocent about what women
really want.

And it's true that when we say no, sometimes we mean
yes. But what if we're drinking, or crying, or rebelling?
There is a difference between a sober yes and the yes that is
self-destructive.

And when we say yes, but not that? *No me gusta.* Why
didn't Kobe understand the difference between pain and
pleasure? And what about I've changed my mind, because
you're scaring me? A yes that becomes a no. Even if we don't
say this out loud, but with our hands and whimpers.

I see Kobe all the time. A possessive arm around our

shoulders. A kiss in public we don't want. A big hand sneaking a pinch or caress when we least expect it. A husband or boyfriend slowly forcing us to open *las piernas* at night whispering *ándale, mami…*

Why don't we complain? Right away?

Well, now I have.

Kobe
had a rape
accusation
ppl dont know/use
him as rapist.

A NATION ADDICTED

San Antonio Express-News • *Mar 23, 1997*

So who's winning the drug war? I want to know! Mexico is like a big *piñata* exploding with *narcoscándalos*, while the United States holds the big certification stick with *muchos pesos*. President Clinton has decided to give Mexico another *chansita*, while Congress is smoking with indignation.

If everyone were sober, I think we might agree that we have to cooperate with Mexico—because the drug lords are beating at our doors faster than you can "just say no."

Ay, how we like to say that Mexico is corrupt. It makes us feel so superior. But in this so-called drug war, that's not the point. We started it. Mexico just got caught in the middle. And we're the only ones who can end it.

Because the American family is in serious denial when it comes to drugs. From our very own president, to someone we love, we all know someone who has used or is using drugs. My brother Jorge will be in prison forever due to his cocaine addiction. My younger brother, Carlos, died tragically from an illness related to his long history of drugs and alcohol. My sister Leticia has used heroin to her shame. Drugs have devastated my family. We will never be the same. But my family, unfortunately, is not the exception.

Now that you know something of my story, please indulge me. No matter how much we try, we simply can't escape drugs because the enemy is us. That is the temptation and subsequent risk of addiction that makes us so human. Most of us have battled some kind of hunger in our lives and lost. Too many of us eat to forget. Others smoke or drink and can't have a good time without it. We seem to tolerate these excesses, few of us are immune. Let's face it—we're in trouble.

We are the richest nation in the world, and we consume drugs like candy. According to joint studies by the U.S. and Mexico, 72 million Americans, or 34% of us, have used drugs at some time in our lives. Call Mexico what you will, but they are not druggies—yet. Only 2 million Mexicans have used drugs, which is about 4 percent of the population.

Thankfully, their morals, and/or their poverty, makes drug use one American habit they have yet to imitate.

And our drug addiction is increasing. According to a survey by the International Narcotics Control Board, cocaine use among young people more than doubled from 1994–1995. Abuse of marijuana and alcohol also rose, even as law enforcement and drug seizures increased. Our 3.6 million addicts created millionaire drug lords.

The rest of the world supports our bad habits gladly, as they are so much poorer than us. Because of our expensive tastes, we have turned their rain forests into golf courses, pristine beaches into tourist trash, exotic animals into endangered species, etc., etc., etc. You get the picture.

The thing is we can't ask Mexico to *Just Say No!*, while we are saying *Yes!* Because it's all about money. That's the addiction we haven't kicked. Everyone I know in Mexico wants to be rich just like the *americanos.*

We have everything. Compared to them. Drugs just happen to be the easiest way to get rich in a place like Mexico. How are you gonna put food on the table, or pay your mother's hospital bills? It's so easy to start, impossible to stop.

I predict that this drug war is gonna be worse than Vietnam. Because, in this war, we stand to risk the democracy that we want for Latin America, and thus test our own. We are so addicted to money that we have seduced every other country with a materialism that has no limits.

For the record, I've never touched drugs. But I do believe we should legalize drugs once and for all. I have no faith that we will change the way we live. It's too hard to quit.

The best gifts are wrapped in love, meaning

SA EV 23 Nov 1999 LUSRICF

It was a piano. Eliberto, my ex-husband, must have saved for at least a year to have it delivered to the house for my 35th birthday. But I didn't understand the gift, and so the piano stood there, lonely, refusing to surrender its secrets. Because I was afraid of the gift.

So many presents. So much to do, so much to wrap. But that's different from "the gift." Do you remember it?

"My children, my friends, my beeper." Most I talked to were silent at first when I asked them what was the best gift they had ever received. But then their eyes jingle-belled, their bodies rustled like expensive wrapping paper as they finally spoke of it. Even the teen-ager Brandon had wanted that beeper so that he could talk to his friends — or maybe his mother.

"The library," Maria found her amigas in books that embraced her when others said she was too different, too lesbian.

Joan named it Jesus when it came in the shape of a white Volkswagen bug after college. Her parents were ministers, and there was no money for new clothes much less a car like that in the '70s. Beep-beep, beep-beep, come out here, her father

Barbara Renaud Gonzalez

yelled to Joan in the house. She kept that car 15 years.

For the skinny-legged Sandra, it was a cheap Thanksgiving jumper with a gold tie from the father who knew that the only daughter was lost in the crowd of brothers. For Carlos, it was Sandra, the gift of the one and only daughter, a slender 13-year thread of more than he thinks he is.

Bill, whose two sons are gifts that take my breath away, says it is knowing who and what you are.

Eduardo says that the biggest gift is the life that his mama gave him. And the people who surround him with their artistic gifts and raunchy laughter and the politics

he doesn't always agree with, though he loves them anyway. Who says some gifts are easy, like the dazzling woman whose gifts torment him, because the best gifts come when you least expect them.

Maybe they come because they're what you really wanted, though you don't dare tell anyone. Those are the mysterious gifts that you can't hold in your hands, but in your heart. And they make us open more and more of our own gifts, so that each one is a little braver than the last.

Maybe it's the jukebox songs that shiver and sway, or maybe it's just the beer and the surprise of that conversation with friends that you know may never be repeated, but Ray already knows what the gift is at the age of 36.

He tells us how he did not have a father and how a football coach saved him. He explains what it is to be young and spinning all over the place like one of those Christmas tops. He was trying so hard, he says, making it, competing, proving himself, that he missed it.

The biggest gift was me, he says. Me. It took him a long time to realize his worth, took him a long time to realize that all that he was, inside, not the outside that

impressed everybody else. Looking back, he says, his youth was like a flower, only he didn't know, and there it faded, almost, like a gift that we don't appreciate because we don't know how valuable it is. Until it's almost too late.

"A flute." Eliberto's gift came because he had heard my story of how my father couldn't afford the piano I wanted, and so had taken out a loan for a flute I could play in the band. It was the cheapest instrument of all, and he compensated for my disappointment by giving me a first-class flute that rested like a pearl necklace in its red velvet case. My father's last payment must have taken the several years it took me to play my first solo.

Later, in college, I had to pawn that flute for $10 because I had no money and nothing to eat. Then I understood.

It took me a long time, but my piano and my flute are always with me. I give them to you. I hope that you will give them to someone else.

Barbara Renaud Gonzalez is a free-lance writer. She can be reached at ExpressLine at 554-0500 and enter 4476.

LOS REGALOS

San Antonio Express-News • Nov 28, 1999

It was a piano. Eliberto, my ex-husband, must have saved for at least a year to have it delivered to the house for my 35th birthday. But I didn't understand the gift, and so the piano stood there, lonely, refusing to surrender its secrets. Because I was so afraid of the gift.

So many presents. So much to do, so much to wrap. But that's different from "the gift." Do you remember it?

"My children, my friends, my beeper." Most I talked to were silent at first when I asked them what was the best gift they had ever received? But then their eyes jingle-belled, their bodies rustled like expensive wrapping paper as they finally spoke of it. Even the teenager Brandon had wanted that beeper so that he could talk to his friends—or maybe his mother.

"The library." María found her *amigas* in books that embraced her when others said she was too different, too lesbian.

Joan named it Jesus when it came in the shape of a white Volkswagen bug after college. Her parents were ministers, and there was no money for new clothes much less a car like that in the '70s. Beep-beep, beep-beep, come out here, her father yelled to Joan in the house. She kept that car 15 years.

For the skinny-legged Sandra, it was a cheap Thanksgiving jumper with a gold tie from the father who knew that his only daughter was lost in the crowd of brothers. For Carlos, it was Rebecca, the gift of the one and only daughter, a slender 13-year-old thread of more than he thinks he is.

Bill, whose two sons are gifts that take my breath away, says it is knowing who and what they are.

Eduardo says that the biggest gift is the life that his mama gave him. And the people who surround him with their artistic gifts and raunchy laughter and the politics he doesn't always agree with, though he loves them anyway. He says some gifts are easy, like the dazzling woman whose gifts torment him, because the best gifts come when you least expect them.

Maybe they come because they're what you really wanted, though you don't dare tell anyone. Those are the mysterious gifts that you can't hold in your hands, but in your heart. And they make us open more and more of our own gifts so that each one is a little braver than the last.

Maybe it's the jukebox songs that shiver and sway, or maybe it's just the beer and the surprise of that conversation with friends that you know may never be repeated, but Ray already knows what the gift is at the age of 36.

He tells us how he did not have a father and how a football coach saved him. He explains what it is to be young and spinning all over the place like one of those Christmas tops. He was trying so hard, he says, making it, competing, proving himself, that he missed it.

The biggest gift was me, he says. Me. It took him a long time to realize his worth, all that he was. Inside, not the outside that impressed everybody else. Looking back, he says, his youth was like a flower, only he didn't know, and there it faded, almost like a gift that we don't appreciate because we don't know how valuable it is. Until it's almost too late.

"A flute." Eliberto's gift came because he had heard the story of how my father couldn't afford the piano I wanted, and so he had taken out a loan for a flute I could play in the band. It was the cheapest instrument of all, and he compensated for my disappointment by giving me a first-class flute that rested like a pearl necklace in its red velvet case. My father's loan payment must have taken the several years it took me to play my first solo.

Later, in college, I had to pawn that flute for $10 because I had no money and nothing to eat. Then I understood.

It took me a long time, but my piano and my flute are always with me. I give them to you. I hope that you will give them to someone else.

WE MUST SEARCH
THE AMERICAN SOUL TO FIND
THE MEXICAN CONSCIENCE

Los Angeles Times • *May 5, 1991*

Pass the *salsa*, please. It's time for the yearly celebration of a Mexican holiday we can actually pronounce—*Cinco de Mayo*—the Fifth of May—with its bounty of *fajitas, sombreros* and *mariachis*.

Forget the reason for the celebration—the battle for independence from the French in 1862. The French were in Mexico for only six years anyway, and left as quickly as they came. Besides, the puppet Emperor Maximiliano was executed, and his wife, Carlota, went crazy in Europe. The great Indian president of Mexico, the Lincolnesque Benito Juárez, preserved the nation, and vindicated Mexican dignity on this day. So let's eat.

There are festivals, parades, the ubiquitous *puestos*, icy *margaritas* and border buses with tourists. Everybody is full to the brim with Mexican culture—processed Mexican culture, anyway.

Our American propensity for adopting culture is ceaseless. We acquire the trappings of the ethnic—the spiritual *retablos* and saints, and turquoise drops, the Spanish red roofs. We visit the Paseo of the Arboretum, the suburbs of Las Colinas, the *fiestas* of summer. While Eduardo Mata's Dallas Symphony serenades and Paul Mejía's Fort Worth Ballet dances, we cross cultural borders every day.

But as we continue to acquire, to feast and market a culture, we deny the existence of the culture's guardians—

those Mexican people who have become aliens on their own indigenous American land, or "illegal aliens." The heart of the political questions regarding immigration, language, representation, education, cannot be solved with a plate of hot *nachos*.

We must search the American soul to find the Mexican conscience.

The problem with the borders of culture is that there are no borders. The only borders are in the mind and in the heart. To the person of Spanish-speaking ancestry, the whole Latin American world is his or her universe. If his mother wasn't born in Mexico, then his grandfather came during the Revolution, or the family remembers Texas before the Alamo. *Sí.*

As we salute the *Cinco de Mayo* holiday, we should consider the meaning of mutuality offered by such a celebration. The psychologist C. G. Jung pointed out that "the power of meaning is curative," or that if we try to understand, and attempt a real consideration of our mutuality as neighbors, then we can really heal so many battle scars.

Culture is not just pleasurable and entertaining, but in its deepest purpose, it is redemptive and restorative, critical and empowering, according to art historian Lucy Lippard. As a society in a wash of transition, we must examine and not just acquire the cultural effects that divide us. If we are to embrace and fuse into the best the world has to offer, then our tourism must go beyond *margaritas* and *machismo*. We must provoke new bonds that can be made only with a scrutiny of what divides us. The dialogue at its most difficult must begin today, not *mañana*.

I like hearing my friends' funky *adiós, amigo,* to Arnold Schwarzenegger's *hasta la vista*, baby, to Madonna's "La

Isla Bonita." Yet, few of us are beautifully bilingual, or have discovered the intricacy of Mexican thinker Octavio Paz, the winner of the Nobel Prize for literature, or the Chilean Pablo Neruda, the world's poet. At a time when the fluency of multi-language is the coin of peace, we are still struggling with the earliest paces of bilingual instruction.

We stand with an "English-only," or "English-first" policy, as if English will lose ground in the rush of such Spanish. Since so few of us are really bilingual, it's hard to convince the Americans on this side of the border that both languages can be trusted—one as the language of the marketplace and one for romance.

Language is a bridge to culture. Consider the language of President Benito Juárez as he responded to the French Maximiliano's naive occupation of Mexico: "It is given to men, Sir, to attack the rights of others, to take their property, to attempt the lives of those who defend their liberty, and to make of their virtues a crime, and their own vices a virtue; but there is one thing which is beyond the reach of perversity, and that is the tremendous verdict of history. History will judge us."

On May 15, 1867, the Emperor Maximilian surrendered in Querétaro, ending the brief residence and tempestuous intervention of the French which had begun in December of 1861. Maximiliano was executed. *Cinco de Mayo*, as the date of heroic defense in the early stages of French encroachment from the city of Puebla, became the standard for Mexican dignity. As Mexico had won her independence from Spain and repelled the American invasions, so had she ousted the French. And rescued her pride.

Cultural pride is a fragile commodity. It is not something that can be bought and sold in the common marketplace, but must be treasured, savored, respected. Culture isn't transportable in the restaurant's "border buses," when the typical American policy is to suppress, denigrate, or reject the typical Mexican face of ambition. A museum floor cannot protect it. One symphony director cannot save it.

Cultural acquisition becomes cultural racism when it caricatures our revolutionary heroes, manipulates our language and trivializes our battles for a restaurant meal. We must begin to search our cultural borders consciously, directly, and *con mucho respeto.*

Our American present will not forgive us. Our Mexican past demands it. And the future will assuredly judge us.

Adelante.

cul' appreciation vs cul racisma?

TEXAS GOVERNOR, NO AMIGO

San Antonio Express-News • Feb 7, 1999

I've never met him, *el* governor, George W. Bush. Thanks to many of the Latinos who voted for him, he is now thinking of the White House.

And I am thinking of killing myself.

He doesn't deserve our admiration, much less our vote. Instead, he has used his magical Spanish to seduce Latinos who are desperate to be part of a Texas that is ours to begin with.

Have you been to a public school lately? In the inner-city? Bush attended the most exclusive schools in the country, and yet he is proposing a $2 billion tax cut on property taxes because he says that the majority of the voters don't want to pay any more for public schools.

He's sensitive to taxes because it was through a sales tax increase, along with the condemning of private land, that he received almost $15 million from an investment of $600,000 for the Texas Rangers Stadium in Arlington. Savvy? He pays *nada* for his vacation home in the fancy Henderson County Rainbo Club. He got an exemption.

And let's talk about diversity, because I am one of those for whom that word is necessary. It is in the public schools where that word has meaning, as rich and poor, Black, White and Brown kids mix together. This ideal used to be called the foundation of our democracy because it teaches our children to respect each other as equals. A difficult process, but it is the best education money can buy.

This dream, I can tell, has been abandoned for the realities of class privilege, marked by suburban flight and the rise of private schools. I never thought that Texas would become like Mexico this way.

That's why we need affirmative action, which is only a Band-Aid for the inequity of our schools. But the governor won't have it. Texas will be almost 50% Latino in 2030, yet Bush never, *jamás*, advocated for minority students when the Hopwood decision ended affirmative action in the state's public and private universities. Even his own appointees to the UT Board of Regents declared their opposition to Hopwood.

Tell me, governor, how can a student compete at the University of Texas unless they've had a decent preparation? Of course, one can go to Yale if the grandfather is a senator in that same state, *¿qué no,* guv?

It also helps to have a congressman-father if you're eligible to go to Vietnam, but you somehow end up in the Texas Air National Guard Unit in 1968. That's when a lot of my friends came back in body bags.

A little affirmative action, maybe? Well, we wouldn't need it either if the schools were fair. They sure wanted Latinos for Vietnam. But you wouldn't know about that.

Yet our governor likes Tejano music and "breaks" the Spanish that we can barely speak with any fluency because it has been denied us. He has reached out to Mexico, like the way he invited six Mexican governors to his recent inauguration, something Ann Richards never did. It's about money, *gente.*

Bush is friendly to Mexico because he realizes the profits—from NAFTA, in particular, that are at stake. He understands that his country wants a free border for capital, for trade, but not for labor or for people. And it is those *maquiladoras*, paying about $1.00 an hour, which isn't even minimum wage for Mexico, that are making *mucho dinero* for U.S. corporations and the Mexican elite.

Those six governors represent the entrenched interests of the Mexican upper-class, the result of Mexico's tragic history of colonialism. But who wants to talk about that? To put it simply, there is no such thing as free trade when one side is rich and the other is poor.

It is the misery of poverty that forces people to cross the border. Especially since NAFTA. And the increased immigration has led to an antagonism towards Mexicans and to those of us who look different. I have never heard the governor protest the fences, the barbed wire, the INS interrogating me at the airport in McAllen.

And, like slow poison, it was the inevitable presence of U.S. Marines in West Texas that led to the shooting death of Ezequiel Hernández, the killing of an American by an American soldier. Where was Bush's famous Spanish then?

Ay, but it's the Spanish, isn't it? The glory of hearing *juntos podemos* that hypnotizes us into forgiving his sins. Compassion, diversity, morality, his words stick together like *cajeta*, delicious even if the candy is just brown sugar and milk. Even if "together we can," means we can if we want to be just like him. And forget everybody else.

Bush has mastered the illusion of difference, while everything remains exactly the same. Our skin may be *cajeta*, but he is inviting us to become the worst kind of *gringo*—so we can do to others what has been done to us. This is what he offers us, and we gladly fall on our knees because we have been so hungry for so long.

He has noticed us, and we happily swallow his *cajeta*.

II.
NO TE DEJES/
MY LINE IN
THE SAND

THREE THOUSAND POLKITAS

For those who have died in Iraq

I know they're out there
Though I've never met them
Lately I've imagined them
at the HEB buying potato chips
The girlie-ones waiting in line
for a purple pedicure getting a tire fixed
on Culebra or watching the Spurs
at some bar on Roosevelt
Barbacoa with the family on Sundays
A pickup game at Woodlawn, their cellphones
buzzing in hip-hop
Hey vato, hey dude, wazzup, babydoll

Three thousand y más soldiers have died
that makes three thousand mothers desmayándose
three thousand fathers who will never cry in public
three thousand sisters, hermanos, tíos, tías
Primos and carnales, abuelitas, abuelos
Teachers and preachers and secret-keepers
Some had boyfriends too I'm sure
wives, husbands, and babies with
pañales to wear, lacy panties to put away
Trocas and new motorcycles
Puppies and engagement rings
Trophies and favorite blue jeans
to wear when they got back

Over there, on the other side of the world
a place where they've never slurped a Big Red

I figure at least another three thousand
of those they call insurgents
Three thousand women widowed
if you include those caught in the crossfire
or the bombs and the children playing soccer
on the wrong side of the street, pillows waiting
for their dreamers, three thousand hand-me-down
heirlooms, lonely teddy bears and burned-fur
kittens, mother's porcelain dishes, broken
and the father's lime cologne dripping on the floor
as the baker's warm bread rises
for three thousand less from soapy-white slips,
smelling of smoke.
If only it was just three thousand cigarettes.
Three thousand stars that
burned like candles on three thousand
birthday cakes. Three thousand make-a-wishes,
three thousand goodbye kisses and three thousand
prayers for a good life three thousand three thousand
round and round like one of our good-time polkitas
Three thousand songs, three thousand steps,
three thousand three thousand three thousand ways
to say I hate you
I love you I hate you
I love you I
Please
          forgive
                    me.

LET'S PARTY! IT'S 1999

San Antonio Express-News • Dec 26, 1999

Let's party. Because the party is over. If you know what I mean.

'Cause we're takin over the joint.

Call it the millennium if it makes you feel better, with its dumb 100 lists grazing the past.

Not me. I'm gonna call it by its true name, because it's like the future, baby. It's *La Reconquista*.

A thousand years ago, the invaders of the north entered the Valley of Mexico with their monster gods and warrior culture. Over time, they built the fantastic Tenochtitlán, the city on an island, and they took tribute and sacrifices from the peoples they conquered.

The years go by, and we have another conquest in the name of the Alamo.

Now it's our turn. The Highspanics, Lowspanics, Chicanos, Tejanos, you-name-it. Who would have thought my mother's *tortillas* would fly around the globe—not just around my kitchen table?

Who could have predicted that millions would despair at the epic of Henry Cisneros, and millions would marvel at the little story of *The House on Mango Street* in ten languages?

We made it to Harvard all right, but half of us don't finish high school. There is a Latina at the president's elbow, another leads a labor union, and the Pope is still trying to make us obey men. One step forward, two steps back.

No matter, I'm *bien* excited. The history of empire is that the conquerors will fall from the weight of their gold, or their greed. Sooner or later.

But what does that mean? Power, if we seize it.

Imagine, we will have the voting power to force our politicians to spend serious money on education, or to build more prisons. We will have the foreign policy power to push Mexico to distribute her wealth—or no more Cancún.

We will have the economic power to share our *tacos* with those who don't have enough to eat, or to keep them and make some of them richer than ever before.

And we will have the cultural power to build our own kind of Ellis Island on the border, a migrant train from that bridge to Washington State, or we will be able to transform the Alamo into a center for peace instead of war.

In other words, we will have the power to change the world as we know it—or to try to defend ourselves against the next *Conquista*.

What is our dream for the future, or has that been conquered too? I want to talk about the lessons we have learned from all the conquests that have created us. Or do we just plan to take what's left of the American pie—until someone in the next millennium says it's their turn?

Maybe all this is too wild, but there is another world to discover out there, because it had to be.

Buckle-up. Nothing stays the same.

We are a millennial people, says Dr. Tomás Ybarra-Frausto, who is from the *barrios* of this city. I think he means that we embody *carne y hueso*, the story of America. Everything that has happened has branded our faces and sculpted our bones.

But it's the spirit he's concerned with, the memories that linger. You can't see the scars, but it's a good thing we have them. And that's why I have hope that we're not going to repeat the past.

It's no accident that we're here, *tú y tú,* and me, *también,* to write the next chapter of our humanity. Now we get to begin a new story, to create heroes who are different, but who look like us. So that we can change the ending to a happy one.

Salud.

THE WATER GODS
OF SAN ANTONIO

Previously Unpublished • Aug 26, 2002

I think Tlaloc must be angry. The Aztec god of rain is parch-
ing most of the United States, we are fighting with Mexico
over water rights, the Río Grande that defines the border between us and Mexico is fading, the Guadalupe is shrinking
and our eastern coastline is one of the dirtiest in the country. But here in San Antonio, Texas, where I live, it rained this
summer like a prophecy straight out of the Bible. Have we
done something wrong?

While Texas is often portrayed as dust-bitten, San Antonio, as one of the ten largest cities in the country, is cursed by
a godsend of water. Situated between the bluebonnet hills of
Central Texas and the sandpipers of the Gulf Coast, San Antonio is blessed by the Edwards Aquifer, the city's only source
of drinking water, a jade-green crescent which cuts a swath
through six neighboring counties, 800,000 acres and roughly
240 miles that generates springs, feeds rivers and lakes, and
dissolves the subterranean limestone into tourist-laden caves.

Which is why the people of San Antonio are in revolt. In
a thirsty protest to a private developer's proposal to build a
PGA-affiliated golf resort on the recharge zone of the fragile
underground aquifer, a striking coalition of civic organizations have banded together and collected a record-shattering
107,032 signatures to force a referendum in November on a
9–2 City Council vote that supported the developer, Lumbermen's Investment Corporation, over passionate opposition.
Mayor Ed Garza, a subject of a *New York Times* story last year
on the hot and spicy *políticos* to watch, garnered only 59,000

votes by comparison.

Access to water was critical to frontier expansion in Texas. The San Marcos springs, called Canocanayesatetlo by the Tonkawan Indians, travelled down the canals, the *acequias* from San Pedro springs to San Antonio, and provided ample water for the irrigated *obrajes,* the fields located between the springs and what is today the city center. The Franciscans established several missions along the San Antonio River, including the Alamo, a symbol of the Texas battle for independence from Mexico. The springs were an important stop for the Spanish Camino Real, the Chisholm cattle trail, and a source of wealth for the Germans who built a dam and then a variety of mills. Now Aquarena Springs is an important tourist destination where in the past you could see frolicking underwater mermaids and even a swimming pig! Though I like to think that the tourists are coming to enjoy our famous Riverwalk shaded by the Cypress trees that grow there because they like to keep wet while sipping icy *margaritas.*

Just so you understand what *agua pura* means to us.

The Battle for Pure Water/*Agua Pura*

"The time comes when public opinion explodes," says former city councilwoman María Antonietta Berriozábal, spiritual force behind the determined coalition known as Save the Aquifer. Thanking the 1,000 volunteers who walked in the blazing heat to gather signatures in two separate and punishing drives after the first set of petitions were deemed insufficient by the City Clerk's office, Berriozábal is a leader in the citizen's rebellion against the subsequent urban sprawl that has been "par for the course" in San Antonio. The Tiger Woods-styled resort, to be developed by Lumbermen's Investment Corporation, was scheduled to create a tax-authori-

ty district, siphoning $52 million dollars to continue impov-
erishing the city, and risk polluting the water, she says.

"What most people don't know," writes Kathleen Dean
Moore in the environmentally conscious *Orion Magazine*, is
that we are facing a "global water crisis as the world's supply
of fresh water is depleted and degraded, and private corporations steadily gain control of what clean water remains." In
another two decades, she predicts, two-thirds of the world's
population will go thirsty.

And while the politicians tout the economic advantages
of a golf resort for tourism, Cambridge University professor
Partha Dadgupta asserts that water is becoming more valuable than diamonds because of its scarcity. The supply has
been so great that the price was zero, he says in the current
issue of the same magazine. Perversely, "the demand for
water has increased greatly as a result of population growth,
rising prosperity, green lawns and golf courses, while the
supply has remained constant." He believes that governments
should support the results of nature's work with cash on the
table. That means conserving watersheds for water purity,
but also wetlands for flood control and forests for climate
stabilization and biodiversity.

The Jordan, the Ganges, and the Nile. Lake Manasarovar
in Tibet. Peru's Titicaca. The Thames, the Amazon, El Lago
de Pátzcuaro, the Hudson River and the Río Grande that isn't
brave or grand anymore. Water is imbued with mythological,
religious, and cultural meanings throughout the world: The
Roman Baths, the washing of the hands known as the *netilat
yadahim* in the Jewish tradition, the *hammam*, the Muslim
sweat bath, the Hindu pilgrims' ritual bathing at prominent
tirthas that mark the river's path, the sacred sweat lodge of
the Native Americans, the Christian *bautismo* and its eternal
symbol of fish.

Water, describes the writer Nataniel Altmas, is at once sustenance, cleansing, initiation, healing, wisdom, enchantment.

But in San Antonio, water is war.

"There has already been incredible growth over the Edwards Aquifer recharge area," says Berriozábal, who almost won the mayoralty herself in 1991, but unlike Garza, without the support of the developers.

Among the early inhabitants of Mexico, creation was the result of the powerful forces of fire and water, and it was Tlaloc who presided over Earthly Paradise. But it was the Aztec water goddess Chalchiuhtlicue who is believed to be responsible for the birth of the first man and woman.

Maybe it is she who brought the rains that flooded us, taking our lives, spilling blood and water on the freeways and purpling the skies for days on end. So that we won't forget.

WHITE FEAR OF
A BROWN NATION:
CHALLENGING HUNTINGTON

*University of Texas at San Antonio Presentation at the
Hispanic Challenge Symposium • Apr 30, 2004*

I am not a scholar. So I'm not going to talk about the content of Huntington's article. I'm interested in the meaning of what he said.

When I was growing up in Texas in the sixties, Texas looked and smelled different. Brown people were just 5% of the population. Now we are one-third, and the largest minority in cities like Dallas where Latinos have become the largest majority/minority. This is rocking the city forever.

I remember—just 25 years ago—when there weren't any "mainstream" Mexican restaurants in Austin except Matt's El Rancho. I didn't grow up listening to Spanish-language radio because it didn't exist north of San Antonio—we used to hear the broadcasts from Mexico City on a clear night in the Panhandle, near Lubbock. *16 de Septiembre* celebrations weren't ubiquitous. There was no *Cinco de Mayo* or *Museum Tesoros* exhibits or lowrider shows or Guadalupe Cultural Arts Centers or Tejano Conjunto Festivals—except in San Antonio. No cultural centers, for sure, and there were no bilingual signs anywhere. Though there were streets in Spanish everywhere.

Texas has changed, yes, because of immigration in particular in the last twenty-five years, but the real changes aren't these brown faces. It isn't JLo or the *tres leches* ice cream, either. Though it's a manifestation.

The real changes are the Mexican American Legal Defense and Educational Fund (MALDEF), Willie Velásquez and the Southwest Voter Registration and Education Project (SWVREP); A Latino mayor and a Latina in Congress. High-risk work. We end up wrestling, scrambling, filibustering—all for equality, often losing, overwhelmed and all too often seduced by "Whiteness" in the process. And the many fights into one long war of inclusivity and a new political and cultural paradigm. One lawsuit after another, one step forward, two steps back, like our *polkitas*. Sometimes three steps. Back. Like Edgewood and public education. The PGA Golf battle.

So you see, the real *cambio* is the one you can't see or hear or taste, but feel: It is the past claim on democracy incarnated by the Civil Rights Movement and the Brown and Black sacrifices in Vietnam.

This is what Huntington fears. It's not the immigrant's lack of English or *barbacoa* on the 4th of July—he is afraid of the twined struggle between the veteran's children and the immigrant's children. And this time there are a lot more of us than in the sixties.

But.

It depends.

In Dallas, years ago when Vicente Fox of Mexico was testing the waters for his presidential run, the immigrants here were polled, and guess what? You think they voted for the PRD—the progressive party? No! They voted for the PAN, the party of the Mexican elite. That's right. The poor struggling *inmigrante* voted on the side and for the *patrones*. And in Mexico, of course, Fox, the former president of Coca-Cola, from the most Catholic of all regions, Guanajuato, Gto., México, became the president!!

Why? Because we are a conflicted people, I think. We are individual moralists because of our Catholicism—not unlike Protestantism. My immigrant mother, after all, voted for Reagan because he used the word "family" and he was anti-abortion. *¡Pero, mija,* he's like us!

I am not concerned with what Huntington says—but what he cannot say. And it is this: Immigrants from the South come from oligarchical, militaristic, traditions. That experience doesn't change the moment they cross the border. A civil society is elusive to them—many immigrant leaders, as the activist Antonio Cabral pointed out to me once, don't have a problem with the Patriot Act. They have never been recognized as equals, and in a society where the Civil Rights Movement made Whites guilty, if not shrewd, about tokenism, especially when it serves a prevailing interest to play Black against Brown—an invite to the Texas A&M Board of Trustees means that everything must be alright. This is Republican up-from-the-boot-straps Lionel Sosa's model.

But here's the *detalle*.

We also crave social justice because of what we've suffered. The Mexican Revolution. A million died in that war, one-tenth of the country's people. And another million witnessed Subcomandante Marcos and the Zapatista Army arrive in Mexico City as a victory for Indigenous Rights. Some of the *mexicanos* and *centroamericanos* and *colombianos* who have come here are here because they've suffered, from persecution and torture. Political resistance. They can be influenced.

When I've talked to immigrant parents in classrooms and on the radio, I find that—because my mother is Mexican and because of ingrained attitudes toward my "status" as a college graduate—I can influence them. Where they might be leaning towards vouchers and private schools, I appeal to their democratic ideals—like public schooling—and minimum wages means something when I explain labor rights as part of the fabric of social struggle in this country. I can even talk about abortion as the difficult democratic journey toward respect for women when a post-modern society refused to take care of children and the father—who has been imprisoned or is unemployed or underemployed—cannot support them. And who owns the media, anyway, that tells men that women are for one thing only?

In other words, if I explain progressive ideas in the context of a collective struggle toward justice, my *gente* gets it.

Make no mistake, Huntington is a warrior-scholar. Funded by right-wing think tanks like the one that funded "The Bell Curve." He is a former director of security planning for the U.S. National Security Council and he has had a distinguished career dedicated to national security, military strategy and global politics. One of his many books, *The Soldier and the State*, says fellow writer Roberto Lovato, is required reading for many aspiring officers like those in the Salvadoran military who implemented NSC operative Huntington's advice in the late 70s and early 80s.

Huntington, brandishing words like civilization and democracy, doesn't know the meaning of those words. He means superiority and power.

He fears the immigrant's children who can make this country understand those words.

He fears us. Me. You. The few of us here—because we have the potential to reach the immigrant.

That's right. The children of immigrants who learn about Martin Luther King and Malcolm X and César Chávez and Toni Morrison and Jessica Hargrove and Thomas Jefferson and Edwidge Danticat and the Bill of Rights and the Women's Movement and Stonewall and Saul Alinsky and listen to hip-hop and Esteban Jordán and somehow put it all together and realize that this country was born to be something other than White.

Huntington is afraid of a true democracy. He comes from a world, like the Bronx, that exists no more. And he wants it back. Just like the seventeen White men that María Antonietta Berriozábal talks about—remembering a Texas where people like me worked in the fields and only dreamed of having daughters like me or better.

We must shape a new society that represents all that we know, and this Huntington article tells me that the time is now. And that is what I'm interested in. Not defense. Offense.

How? We need, says Lovato, and I agree with him, a sustained critique of "White Fear." We must develop a musical, political, cultural and literary critique of Whiteness.

You see, the immigrant represents the symbolic border to democracy. And we must dismantle White Fear so that we can all cross into this—promised land.

THE EDUCATION
OF THE HEART

Gracias for inviting me…I think.

You see, I am rather *avergonzada* to be here today. *No lo merezco*. I have never been to a college graduation in my life—and have sworn to my friends that I would never ever attend one. They're so boring!

And here I am. Humbled, and now *la Virgen* is testing me—by giving me a chance to say what I always knew should be said, and that I could do it better!

As the first college grad in my family, my parents were on their way to the bank to borrow money to come to my graduation at Pan American in Edinburg [now the University of Texas Río Grande Valley]. My mother had two jobs then—she was a restaurant cook in Beeville and a nurse's aide at night. My father worked for an oilfield company in Corpus, and me, as the oldest of eight, seemed to always be in debt. My parents were already planning on borrowing more money to buy my five brothers their first matching shirts and ties and I couldn't confess to them that I also needed about $11 for my cap and gown rental on top of that. It didn't seem fair to me—so I fast-talked my parents out of it. Told them it didn't matter, that it was a waste of time—but of course I wanted to celebrate in some way.

I know now that I wanted something exactly like this *Despedida*.

I want to talk to you about what I've learned since the many college graduations—my own and others—I didn't go to. *Quiero compartir* the education that really matters—the one with no ceremony or paper or commencement.

It's the education that is hardest of all—and the most expensive—but it's the only one that really matters and unfortunately, we learn too little about on a college campus. And I think it's the one we really want—the one we are seeking and I hope that what we've found here—is a way to that other one.

I'm talking about love.

Especially on this day, Mother's Day, the woman in whose arms we first learned the meaning of that word. It is through the quality of her love that we learn how to love her, another being, ourselves, others, and finally, the rest of the world. Without this complete education, we go through life searching and searching—you see people piling on degrees or medals or prizes or lovers or food or fancy cars or jewelry—all in the hope of getting love in return.

This need for love is what makes us human. It propels us forward, pushing us sometimes to great accomplishments and forcing others, or seducing others, to pay attention to us. And then we want those people to love us exactly for who we are.

It is from this *corazón*, I think, that we can create and shape our future. And therefore the world's. It is from this ripened and fruitful *corazón* that we can find the truth which will give us the courage and resilience to change the world that we now have. A world of wars and physical materiality that is an illusion of success, of progress, of development.

But that has nothing to do with love.

I know that as students in Mexican American Studies you have learned about Aztlán, our geographical and spiritual homeland. Since the sixties, the birth of the Chicano Movement, we have invoked the ancestors who walked to

Tenochitlán, present-day Mexico City, through Texas and the Southwest in claiming our right to America, to being here on this land, demanding respect for our people and our language and culture.

We come from people who were educated in ways that many MBAs and MSWs and MDs and Ph.Ds hunger for— but few attain. It is an education that seems simple, but in this post-modern era is almost impossible. Our indigenous ancestors shared everything they had because they loved each other. This generosity included—the greatest mother— Mother Earth herself.

And in a world so uneducated in loving our ecology and the spirit, our ancestral love of earth and each other, can save us and the planet.

Remember the battle over the Edwards Aquifer last year? And how over a hundred thousand signatures were collected in the summer's *comalazo* protesting a golf course development over the Aquifer?

It was called progress, wasn't it? And the development is beginning, despite the protests from so many citizens. Why? Because Lumbermen's, the developer, convinced COPS [Communities Organized for Public Service and Metro Alliance are a coalition of congregations, schools, and unions]—a critical sector of our community—that good jobs were at stake, which outmaneuvered the constitutional right of citizens to vote.

What's a good job to COPS? Jobs that require a long commute north, to support a golf resort built over one of the world's most productive aquifers—and the city's only source of drinking water?

You wouldn't know it from the reportage coming from the *San Antonio Express-News*—which is a big business paper—but water is predicted to be as precious as diamonds

in the next twenty years, which means that we are risking a
diamond field that could bring real prosperity to this area
and water to the world. Instead we are giving it away to
some very rich people who may pollute it if they don't sell it
back to us in bottles and at prices that could very well keep
your children and grandchildren thirsty and in debt for
many generations to come.

Texas is one of the most polluted states in the country.
The Gulf Coast, one of the ten dirtiest waters in the nation.
The Río Grande is a *río feo*, nothing like its majestic past,
when ferries would travel it from New Orleans. Most of
us have allergies and sinus problems. Why? Because of the
poverty of the air. I don't have a car, so I walk from Hilde-
brand and Fredericksburg to downtown, and I can smell the
earth sweating in its misery of fumes and salt and sugar.

Walking gives me a whole different experience of the
world. For one, I know the moon's cycle, and it makes
me happy. But the walking also depresses me—it's like
witnessing closeup how we're doomed in the way we have
abandoned and shut up our *viejitos*. I walk past history
every day and it's amazing to me that we say we respect
our grandmothers, but not the neighborhoods they once
knew. And the trees? Even on some of the most elegant
neighborhoods and streets like Mary Louise, or my own,
Club, you would be surprised how many yards don't have
shade. Why should they? People take their cars three blocks
to the grocery store—we now have only one kind of grocery
store—which is covered in concrete to accommodate the
cars.

What we eat from these stores is another subject en-
tirely. Dr. Roberto Jiménez, who is Professor José Jiménez's
brother and a health care leader in Bexar County, says that
our diabetes rate is four times higher than Whites. He told

me in a panic that physicians are seeing diabetes in children at a previously unheard of—six years old! They are literally overwhelmed at the economic and health consequences for our society. It's like knowing that we're going to be attacked by terrorists and not doing anything. And we're the terrorists and the terrorized at the same time.

And yet we celebrated the Toyota's plant coming to San Antonio, ¿verdad? That's a sign of progress, right? What kind of progress?

According to the EPA, the average fuel economy of our cars and trucks fell to its lowest level in two decades. While petroleum is a finite resource according to many experts— Iraq has one of the world's most productive oilfields in the world—and we are not the only customers, but one of many… See the connection to the war?

Cars and light trucks—SUVs, pickups—isn't that why the Toyota plant is coming here? Together they account for 40% of the nation's oil consumption and a fifth of the carbon dioxide emissions, which many scientists see as the leading contributor to global warming. Which causes allergies. Our dependence on cars means we can live in suburbs without old trees and with long commutes which burn up more gasoline and prevents us from walking, which is the difference between obesity and our health, and the health of our cities.

You call this an educated society?

At the downtown Y the other day I asked Cristina, a UTSA student who graduates this summer, what she really wanted to hear someone talk about. Her answer was a question that surprised me.

What is truth?

I had several sleepless nights thinking of her question and realized this is why I had gotten my second chance to go to a graduation. Ok, ok! So you want the truth, Cristina?

You want me to talk about the fiction of your beautiful education? Our shiny paper identity? That is something we cling to in a culture that won't respect us for who we are? You want me to let you believe, as I did for way too long after I received my degrees, that I was actually worth something because I had spent a few years in a classroom?

The truth is that there are few lies as big as the one that you are a better person because of your college degree. If that was the case, we wouldn't have death row or the homeless or abandon our mothers and fathers in nursing homes. Or go to war. I've seen many friends who are worse off, not financially, but emotionally, with their college degrees hanging on the living room wall.

That's because learning about love is an education of the heart, and there are no classrooms for that. It's a university of one. A college education means that you have absorbed some facts, data, statistics, mastered some new words, formulas. It prepares us to live in a world where competition and material gain rule.

But a college education cannot prepare us for the internal world where the heart and the spirit rule. That's a world that our ancestors knew very well and that is the education I think Cristina really wants, though I can't promise any material wealth or visible rewards.

The only degree we earn from this lifelong journey is a glimpse into love as the truth we are seeking. Because few of us get that degree, though we get another chance every day that we are alive on this earth.

What I am learning is that love is freedom. The act of loving frees us from judging ourselves and everyone else—opening us to the possibility of forgiving every single person who has hurt us—for the daily insults and pretensions and the long day's journey into night childhood nightmares. Truth—we are worth being loved because we are each uniquely beautiful and special, but so is everyone else. So loving teaches us that every time we call someone a name—on the freeway, *negro* to the person living on the other side of town, *joto* to a man who walks funny, or *esa gente baja* who don't have as much "education" as you—we lose a chance at learning what we are here on earth for.

And so we become a little less human.

These are some of the truths that our ancestors understood, and unfortunately, they are not the truths that we invest so much time with in school. But if you have hunger and ambition, as I did, to learn something about yourself because you are in this essential program, then I trust that you are seeking something far more important than a piece of paper.

What I'm trying to tell you is that you have inherited the potential to rescue the world. It is in our memories, in the bones of our faces, in our diabetic genes and in the compassion our mothers and fathers taught us, who have suffered so much to get you to this place.

They wanted you to get an education because they didn't want you to suffer the way they have, but what I want you to know is that now *I want you to suffer.* I hope you really suffer.

Suffering, you see, can be very good for you. Because in suffering there is a chance you will become compassionate about the rest of the world that is truly suffering. And from that common ground, you may learn what love is about— from the people who ride the bus with me in San Antonio to the people of Palestine and Afghanistan and Iraq because now you might get a glimpse, a sour taste, of what they go through every day.

So they are human after all. So they do have dreams just like you and me. And we depend on the same round rock of Earth, don't we?

You, the children of Aztlán, have to suffer—because your life will be much more intricate and vexing than even mine has been—in order to create a consciousness—a *conciencia* for the world.

My mother, before she died, wanted me to cross new borders with the valor that she crossed from Mexico to the United States, alone, when she wasn't even eighteen yet. But she couldn't foresee how many more borders I had to cross and when she would complain, I had to remind her that she was the one who raised me to cross every border I saw. What I have realized is that I am my mother's daughter, but never will I be her. I am a Chicana and for me that means I am a citizen of the world as well.

My hope is that the education you're celebrating today will take you to the one that really matters. Because the one you've finished sometimes gets in the way of finding your heart. But you—no matter the scientific or artistic or political achievements—they won't help you and they won't save the rest of us if you don't also learn to love yourself and everyone on this planet with every cell and ounce and drop of your being.

You want the truth, Cristina? Love is what really matters, and without it, your degree won't mean anything. Don't be afraid to find it. Tell the truth. Honor what you know in your heart to be true. What your mother taught you. Don't compromise. Every time you tell the truth, you will find that you love yourself a little more and that you have just rescued the world a little bit. Love yourself and others the way our *madres* love us: without measure, forgiving and helping and without any boundaries.

I didn't have children, but you are also mine. When I write, I give birth over and over. And I try to find love in the ink and in the flesh of the page. As I am your mother, I give you all the love I have, and pray that you will love more than I have in my past, and that you will love each other and the world so much that one day we will have clean water and fresh air and trees on every block and safe and healthy children and most of all—peace. Love this Mother Earth!

I believe in you. And I love you.

Que la Virgen los bendiga. Feliz Día de las Madres. Gracias.

ESPERANZA CENTER FOR PEACE AND JUSTICE

Z Magazine • *Jan 1, 2001*

They seem to go way beyond what people want their money spent on. That group flaunts what it does—it is an in-your-face organization. They are doing this to themselves.
—Mayor Howard Peak of San Antonio, quoted in *The New York Times* on September 13, 1997, regarding the city council's unanimous vote to completely defund the Esperanza Center.

Over thirteen years ago, a group of progressive women decided to build an organization that would challenge injustice through the vehicles of art and culture. Gay and lesbian rights, U.S. intervention in Central America, labor rights, bilingual education, the environment, women's reproductive rights, tourist culture—it's all the same battle, they concluded. And from the idealism of their youth, the Esperanza Center for Peace and Justice has emerged as a beacon for radical thinkers, activists and artists from around the country. [I worked at the Esperanza Center during this time. For more information, see Virginia Grise's book, *The Panza Monologues*, UT Press 2014.]

Now, that dream has landed them in federal court, where they wait for a decision that may take them all the way to the Supreme Court.

"Because of the Esperanza" (a Spanish word for hope, but it implies the liberation of a people in this context), says writer Sandra Cisneros, there is a real Latino "Left Bank" on the San Antonio River. It is one of the reasons she chose this soulful Mexicanized city as her adopted home. And others keep coming. Among other arts and cultural organizations around the country, the Esperanza has no equal, and is simply the home they've been searching for.

It was therefore inevitable, some people say, that the Esperanza would have to sue the City of San Antonio in a firestorm over the first amendment, decency, and homophobia.

Never popular at City Hall for their political activism fused with artistic programming, the Esperanza was the only arts and cultural organization to lose all of its funding in the summer of 1997. That period, if you remember, was one of Republican attacks on the National Endowment for the Arts (NEA) amidst the furor of obscene art, like the *Piss Christ* by Andrés Serrano, and the chocolate-covered performance nudity of Karen Finley. In this artistic backlash, two conservative councilmen led a *machetazo* that sliced 15% of all the arts programs—under the rubric of long-neglected street repair—in a city that prides itself on its rich cultural heritage.

It is this *mestizaje* of Anglo, Black and Mexican heritage that is the lifeblood of San Antonio. Tourism brings billions of dollars in much-needed revenue, and while visitors enjoy strawberry *margaritas,* chicken *fajitas* and *chipotle salsa* on the city's fabled Riverwalk, much of the Latino population remains impoverished and uneducated. The mythical Alamo is just a few blocks away, still privately managed by the Daughters of the Texas Revolution, as a symbol to many Latinos "of a victory that became a defeat [of the Mexicans]," shrugs Cisneros.

With its five Spanish missions (the Alamo was one), its slew of military bases, the city has been colonized, militarized, and now touristized so that "our culture is for consumption only," says Dr. Antonia Castañeda, a historian at St. Mary's University. The battle for inclusion of Latino arts and cultural organizations alongside the traditional museums and symphony has been hard-won, she explains, from the esteemed Guadalupe Cultural Arts Center to the Esperanza's *MujerArtes*, a women's pottery collective that seeks to create authentic, non-commercialized art from its working-class Tex-Mex origins.

Just prior to its defunding, the Esperanza enjoyed a seven-year track record of grants from the city, and had received the highest rating by a peer review panel which had recommended a total of $76,000, or about half of the Esperanza's total operating budget. During the call for budget cuts, a Christian talk show host, Adam McManus, slammed the Esperanza's gay and lesbian film festival "Out at the Movies." On his radio show, he orchestrated a campaign by the religious right that produced indignant letters and phone calls to the city council. That summer, the Esperanza received death threats. A week's worth of homophobic cartoons, penned by the *San Antonio Express-News'* Nacho Guarache, vilified Graciela Sánchez, the Center's Yale-educated director, and the Esperanza's cause.

"Our mission has always been about giving voice to those who have never had a voice," says Sánchez, who returned to the *barrio* she grew up in. Sánchez has long been labeled by the media as a lesbian, a preference that she confessed to her parents long ago, and one that she says has taught her much about the multiple oppressions facing her community. This is what the Esperanza addresses with its art and cultural programming, she says. Many of the Esperanza's provocative art exhibits and programs have been copied, years later, by major institutions. Many of the struggling artists that the center first promoted are now nationally known, like writer Sandra Cisneros and Puerto Rican balladeer Lourdes Pérez, who has sung with Argentina's Mercedes Sosa.

It is the distinctive character of America's segregation of art and politics that keeps cultural organizations from challenging the very government that funds them. Court cases are expensive, exhausting, and in Texas, a recipe for bankruptcy.

At the Esperanza Center, Amy Kastely, a law professor and former board member, began to work feverishly in that summer of 1997 to organize a team of seven lawyers and former students—all women working pro bono—who were as determined as she was to take the City of San Antonio to federal court.

Working many nights and weekends, the lawyers, led by Kastely, determined that they had a strong First Amendment case—focusing on the "disfavored viewpoints" clause of the constitution. Even more significantly, they believed that it could be a "test case" for arts funding in the wake of the Supreme Court's ruling on Finley v. NEA in 1998. That case, misinterpreted by some, upheld Congress' rights to require the NEA to consider general standards of decency in making funding decisions, but it also said that the government cannot discriminate against groups that promote "disfavored viewpoints." Joined in the lawsuit by two organizations under its fiscal umbrella, the San Antonio Lesbian and Gay Media Project and the small arts group Visual Artists Network (VAN), the Esperanza made four allegations against the city council, all related, and supported, by the First Amendment.

According to Kastely, the city council buckled under pressure from the religious right.

"The First Amendment claim really has to do with whether the city is entitled to pick and choose among arts organizations depending on their viewpoints," says Kastely. Everybody agrees they can pick and choose depending on artistic excellence…the difference in this case is they refused to fund the Esperanza because of the Esperanza's involvement in social justice issues, because of their support for lesbian and gay cultural expression. To say that art and politics is not related, she emphasizes, is "to deny that different cultures have different views...this is viewpoint discrimination.

"And disfavored viewpoints are an obligation imposed by the Constitution."

Besides the First Amendment claim, the Esperanza alleges that the city council sought to "appease public animus" by defunding the Esperanza after an extensive homophobic campaign, they violated the 14th Amendment's equal protection clause, and they conspired to do this out of public view in a back door meeting—in violation of the Texas Open Meetings Act. Finally, Kastely says, the city council punished the Esperanza for daring to file suit against them, by denying their right to apply for funding in the year following their elimination—a violation of the First Amendment's right to petition.

Besides asking the court to reverse the council's decision and to order the city to follow its own merit-based criteria to allocate arts funding, the Esperanza seeks $420,000 in compensation, a sum that includes money the Esperanza estimates it would have received from the city from 1998–2001.

Trial testimony between Mayor Howard Peak and Mary A. Kenney, attorney for the Esperanza, on August 21, 2000

Kenney: What are the social issues that you've heard that they have had programming about?

Peak: I guess primarily gay and lesbian issues. (More questions from Kenney about the city's application process, the Mayor's knowledge of the Esperanza and their "bad publicity.")

Kenney: And you therefore were basing your opinion on what others had told you about the Esperanza, correct?

Peak: Well, not just what others had told me, but what I had heard in the community chiefly through publicity generated by, or as a result of, the organization itself about what the organization did.

(More questioning along this line)

Kenney: And you certainly never went to the Esperanza to ask them about their programming, or to look at it and find out for yourself, did you?

Peak: No.

Scot Powell, a professor of government and law at the University of Texas at Austin, believes the Esperanza has a case.

"You constantly see governmental bodies penalizing 'out' groups for their view," he told the *San Antonio Express-News* on the day before the front-page trial. And you know in a real sense that the government was doing it because they didn't like the group's political views, but the government will say, oh no, not us! To be sure, we didn't approve of their view, but there's lots of views we don't approve of, and we did this for the best of all reasons."

Other legal experts told the *San Antonio Express-News'* Maro Robbins that the answer to the question of tax dollars supporting unpopular art comes from a dispute at the

University of Virginia, when the school denied funding to
a student-run publication because of its religious content.
The Supreme Court ruled in a 1995 decision that because
the university funded all sorts of student publications
without restricting their content, the school could not single
out Christian materials without squelching students' First
Amendment rights.

And, because the City of San Antonio had no limitations
on what kind of groups could apply for arts funding, nor on
what kind of art was produced, "denying one group funds
simply because it espoused social views likely would violate
the Constitution," said David Dittfurth, a constitutional law
professor at St. Mary's University, to the same paper.

The federal trial, expected to last one week in the burning
heat of last August, was condensed to two days in a packed
courtroom filled with grassroots supporters, including
teenagers, labor leaders and the elderly parents of Graciela
Sánchez. Around the city, *Todos Somos Esperanza* banners
and signs blanketed the city with the Esperanza's brilliant
red and gold lettering. "We are all Esperanza," echoed the
members of the Esperanza's street theatre, who performed
their free speech skits across from the city's main cathedral
and at the *plazas. Cafecitos,* or coffee klatches, were hosted
by the rich and poor alike to educate the community about
free speech and democracy.

The night before the trial, a candlelight vigil was held
in front of the Federal Courthouse witnessed by television
cameras and people from the housing projects next door to
the imposing building at the Hemisfair Plaza.

Political observers say the Esperanza can win. But that
is just the beginning of an arduous legal journey toward the
very conservative Fifth Circuit. Carlos Guerra, a metropolitan
columnist with the *San Antonio Express-News,* has predicted

that the city will appeal. They have "an unlimited legal budget…they will cut off their nose to spite their face."

Nine months after the trial, Federal Judge Orlando García, a former legislator and respected member of his legal and hometown community, has still not issued a decision. "It could take many more months…as long as he wants," says Kastely. "His taking time means that he wants to craft something that will withstand an appeal," suggests Judith Sanders-Castro, a Rural Legal Aid lawyer who has litigated in his court before.

"I would think that the evidence they put on is undeniable," she continues. But, she cautions, "how is it that the judge can withstand political concerns in San Antonio…is something else." In San Antonio's conservative climate, she explains, ruling on the side of the Esperanza means that he runs the risk of being isolated from contacts, and losing the fraternity of his peers.

"The Esperanza…has changed the political and social landscape of San Antonio," say the activists who volunteered for the rotating shifts that the trial preparation required. "The judge himself benefited from the social movements of the last generation," they say. "Let's hope he understands that it is the women, *las mujeres,* like Graciela Sánchez and others like her, who have learned from the mistakes of the past…as they seek to change the future."

Judge Orlando García, at the conclusion of the federal trial on August 22, 2001: "Ok. I want to commend, this is one of the best, well-developed cases and argued cases that I've seen in my six years that I've been here."

[The Esperanza Center won their federal lawsuit in 2001 on all four counts.]

THE FORGETTING OF ALBERTO R. GONZALES

The Texas Observer • Jan 21, 2005

Starch, corn *tortillas*, and a pencil. My first day of school. A *mexicanita* in a blue puffy-sleeved dress blooming with Texas wildflowers made from the twenty-pound bags of white flour they used to sell back then, remember? Blue as the Niagara starch my mother used to make my dress shine—poor but clean, you understand. A tablet of Big Chief paper fresh as my crinkling petticoats, and two pencils so thick and fat they felt like butter in my hand.

My story is not so different from many other educated Latinos in Texas—like Alberto Gonzales, I was fortunate to have parents who cared in their *pobreza* about my education. But Gonzales (no relation), the first Latino to be appointed U.S. Attorney General—from San Antonio and Houston, friend and legal counsel to President Bush, Harvard Law graduate—has forgotten where he comes from.

According to his biography, Alberto R. Gonzales had working-class parents, and like me, he was a stellar student who attended the best schools in the country. We comprise the generation of Latinos who were admitted and given financial aid to schools like Harvard because of the Civil Rights Movement in this country—a civil earthquake of protests and riots and Vietnam that forced this country to confront its history of racism and injustice.

It is a history that many would like to forget.

Now, Alberto R. Gonzales has been charged with the responsibility of enforcing those civil rights that took us to the table by a president who has done everything possible to deny them. It's all done with paper and pencil these days instead of rocks and ropes.

My mother sold Chiclets on the streets of San Luís Potosí, and she taught me to never forget what it was like to be poor. Well, for many of us who were able to get a college education because of the Civil Rights Movement, let me tell you—it is very easy to forget. The rewards in this country are for those who put the past behind them. If you work hard and don't remind your bosses too much of where you came from and how much still has to change, you get invited to the mansions. I've been there. And when your brown *carita* is at the table surrounded by the powerful and wealthy and famous, you are so proud knowing that your parents sacrificed all their lives for this. Look at me!

And with all the compliments and invitations because your presence makes the powerful feel less guilty for what they've done to people like our parents, you begin to imagine that you really are more beautiful and brilliant—not just lucky to be at the table. *Poco a poco* you begin to forget.

When Alberto Gonzales was counsel to then-Governor Bush in Texas, he helped Bush conceal a misdemeanor drunk-driving conviction from his dark past. By helping Governor Bush lie when he was called for jury duty. You and I could go to jail for this. Some of us could get deported.

But that was nothing compared to the *indecencia* Gonzales demonstrated in advising Bush who denied clemency in questionable death row cases, contributing to a death row culture that the U.S. Supreme Court has recently rejected as unjust and illegal. A total of 128 executions occurred in Texas during the six-year tenure of Governor Bush; 36 of them happened on Gonzales' watch as Chief Counsel.

In his role as legal counsel to the president, Gonzales was

central to the White House policy to slow-kill affirmative action, and to fast-freeze voter disenfranchisement. He was also central to policies blurring religion with government—which sounds devout but takes us on a slippery road back to the Inquisition. And before the presidential elections last November, more fingerprints: he disregarded new policies recommending federal enforcement of bilingual documents and translators for all government agencies.

So this is what you have to do to be embraced by the powerful in the country? Has the historic denial of civil rights taken our souls too?

Perhaps this is why Gonzales played such a key role in the White House's inner circle shaping anti-terrorism policies denying the most basic civil rights for prisoners of war. Even if we started the war despite what the rest of the world says, even if we can't speak the enemy's language, understand their history. Even if we come from a people who know what it is like to be so forgotten, that your living is one long remembering to what others have done to you.

We are victims of violence unleashing violence in a merciless circus, says the Mexican poet José Emilio Pacheco. With the featured attraction being—Abu Ghraib. Followed by Guantánamo and Afghanistan.

Alberto R. Gonzales has forgotten. Or maybe he can't forget? But I have paper and pencil too. The bluest sky, corn *tortillas* soft as my mother's kiss on that first day of school. Two fat pencils. So that I would give one to the other little brown girl who smelled of corn.

No te olvides, mijita, de donde vienes.

III.
LA FAMILIA

El Borracho

My brother wants to kill himself,
the youngest sister yells at me
from the west coast, and I know

you will do something, you will
save him because you are.
She says because I'm the oldest,

that I must save him again and then she
hangs up.
He is going on binges, he's an alcoholic.

Like Mami was, she means. Hermana is afraid
he will die like my mother.

Chronic alcoholism, the death certificate says.
It means she was drunk, then more rum,
passed out, vomited, and went into a coma.

Do something, Hermana says.
She is so far away.
Then I see my brother on his tricycle, and I'm twelve,

pushing him, it's summer, and he's only two.
I see him tremble, a leaf loosed from the family
tree as the older brother drinks, and drinks,
and dies right after the New Year.

Save him. El borracho tells me that a man molests
him when he's twelve. He means rape, but can't say that.

Drinking when he tells me this. On that summer night,
he drinks maybe a dozen beers and falls asleep.

Now I see him when he was eleven, must have been
before everything happens. Daddy has left, never returns,
and Mami works three jobs to support all of them. Four

boys crying when I get home from college. They begin to hate
me, between the sobs. I don't suffer like them.

Mami starts to drink, and one night my brother tells me
that love is like a beer bottle. Icy cold, and could I please
buy him a six-pack.

He is trying to kill himself, Hermana says.
Do something.

Pass the Turkey

National Public Radio • *Oct 23, 1993*

I knew it was time to leave when the second fight broke out in the bathroom. And the police were afraid to go in. *"Mami,"* I pleaded with my mother. *"Por favor, vámonos."*

But the *cumbia* contest was just beginning. It was midnight on Thanksgiving at La Esquinita. And it was *rockiando*, as they say on the Eastside of Austin. And my mother wanted to dance. Or at least sneak the drinks the men kept buying me.

So this is how I spent my Thanksgiving. It all began the week before when my 60-something, proud-to-be-single Mexican mother called me in Dallas to ask what I wanted with my turkey.

"Pero, Mami, why are we having turkey?" I demanded. We never had turkey when we were growing up—when I wanted to play Pilgrim fathers. *"No, yo quiero un plato de enchiladas con pollo, por favor."*

"No te entiendo, mijita," she says in that superior *interior-de-México* and you are just a *pocha-sinvergüenza* way of hers. "You went to college, didn't you? And that school up north? What did you learn? I'm making *pan,* gravy *con* giblets, cornbread dressing, the green beans Del Monte, cranberry relish, the potato salad too, the Jell-O salad with real fruit cocktail and the pumpkin pie. But I'll make rice and beans on the side, if you want. The boys want their turkey! *Mira,* I am making fifty dozen *tamales* because I know how you love them."

"Engordan." I was insulted by now. They make me fat. "I only use Crisco!" she says. "That's not fat, that's Crisco!"

I still don't understand Thanksgiving. It doesn't translate well into Spanish. When I patiently explained about the Pilgrims to my mother after a third-grade lesson, seeking some confirmation of our role in this event, she reminded me that every celebration has two faces. "*Vaya*," she said. "We don't celebrate it in Mexico…but I'll make you a special *guisado* tomorrow, just for you. And you can have that Trix-are-for-kids you like for breakfast."

Perhaps I realized even then that no amount of turkey would make me belong with the Pilgrim's descendants I sat with at school. Everyone but me seemed to have an ancestor on the Mayflower. Though I knew—I knew—that the sepia skin of Texas with its sunsets strung with a thousand *piñatas* embraced me too. Especially me.

Thanksgiving is not a day of giving, but of taking. We are grateful for another's tradition of generosity. One we cannot ever hope to match. A generosity that I liken to the Mexican *guelaguetza*, that celebration of community founded in an ancient reciprocity that ensures a survival of the people. It is a ceremony of *compadrazco* and more. It recognizes a solidarity that is symbolized with exchanges of the earth's bounty which sustains us.

It is not a day of thanksgiving, but a commitment to each other. That we cannot survive alone.

"Since you value your Mexican heritage," my mother says after our feast, "then you'll go out dancing with me and Alma and Graciela?" "But aren't those *cantinas* dangerous—the kind you hang out at?" I ask, feeling very, very, pale. "I knew it. I know you don't like to be with us because you are not used to this life. You're too high-class. I understand very well. You're different."

"What time should I be ready?" I ask my mother.

So let's celebrate. That we are Americans. And give thanks that there is room at the table for all of us.

I AM MY MOTHER'S HOPES...AND FEARS

San Antonio Express-News • *May 12, 1996*

She crossed the Río Grande from Mexico when she was just 18. She won't tell me how she did it. She was escaping a bad marriage and my old-fashioned grandmother. She was to be my mother.

How she dreamed of having me, her first-born, a daughter. After five years of marriage to my father, she could not conceive, and so she began to search for me. I was in her *caldo*, that succulent vegetable-beef soup that is said to start a baby. She sipped me in the bouquets of tea that promise children from the *curanderas.* Potions, *yerbitas,* prayers and devotions to the holiest mother of all. Yes, my mother made her pleas to the blessed Virgen de Guadalupe so that she too would become a perfect mother.

"No eres madre," I tease her today. *"Eres una fábrica."* You are like a baby factory. After all, she had eight children in 13 years. "You, Bárbara," she would say as we gathered around the kitchen table before Daddy came home. The same table where he would ridicule her supper, her petite body, her English, her Mexican ways.

"You, Bárbara," she would begin her dreaming. "You must travel and write. Leticia, teacher, you have patience. Jorge Antonio, lawyer, keep the rest out of jail. Susanita, the middle child, be the boss once and for all. Daniel, the sick one, you will keep the family together. Carlitos, the charmer, a politician. Roberto, we need a doctor in the family. Esteban, the baby in diapers, you can be the artist and rebel all you want."

My mother took us to church every Sunday and even to
Vacation Bible School in the summers. Every year it was a
different religion, because she was looking for the answer,
and she couldn't seem to find the questions that I would ask
her. "Believe in God," she told us. "Have faith. And I will
take you to the library next week."

She wanted me to be so different. Though Daddy
claimed to be the real brains of the family, it was my mother
who confronted his lack of ambition with her own. "Take
care of your brothers, and watch the *caldo de rez*," she
would say, rushing to her night job as a nurse's aide. "They
are men, after all."

She let me date early, and encouraged me to have a rich
social life in contrast to the restrictions of the girls around
me. She showed me diagrams to my questions of sex. "Here
it is. Don't. Men will never respect you. Believe me, I know.
And have a good time."

My mother surprised me with my first suitcase when I
went away to college. "Remember," she said, "you are no
beauty like your sisters, so you must learn to be independent of men. Men don't like smart women."

When my mother crossed the border in search of a
better life, she didn't realize what she had done. She, who
believes in the tradition of family, now lives alone, divorced
after a marriage of 28 years. She says that she will never
marry again. She says that if she were to do it all over, she
would have left my father in her 30s, and that she was afraid
of nothing after all.

Now she goes dancing on Saturday nights, and to church
on Sunday mornings. She has a wall of college diplomas
from her children. She has survived a son's death and
another's imprisonment. She has seen a daughter return
from prostitution, and she worries about *la feminista* and is

shocked by the one who is lesbian, or both. We are not what she expected, after all. Maybe if my father, Roberto, had been a real father, it would be different, she says. Maybe it's her fault.

My mother says that she may not live long enough to see the youngest, Esteban, receive his Ph.D. She trembles when she says this. Her hands look like wine-soaked bread.

I am the child of my mother's passion, the embodiment of her wildest hopes, and for that she fears what I have become. Know that she is still searching, and that it's up to me to find it. To do that, I will have to cross even more borders. She is me, but I can never be her.

"Come home, *mijita*, she says in the middle of her loneliness. "I will make your favorite *caldo de camarón*."

You have forgotten me.

Remember Mariachis
at My Funeral

Los Angeles Times • *May 10, 2001*

If you saw her on the street, you wouldn't have looked twice.

My mother, Marina.

Marina, *levántate*. A basket of sweet bread with pink-cloud icing at dawn. Boxes of Chiclets tinkling like marbles at the *plaza*. Handmade lady's dresses, starchy, heavy, on her five-year-old arms. She wants to play, but she can't. Her family is starving, it is in the years after the Mexican Revolution, and her mother is sewing, embroidering, crocheting, baking, doll-making, ingenious in the way that poverty forces you to become an artist. Or a warrior.

Her mother says that people buy from her because she's so little, and those prized fat legs. She sings a verse for each sticky *campechana*. Oh, how she makes people laugh and spend, but more than anything she wants to go to school.

But there is no money.

And when she's in the fifth grade, her mother tells her that she is too old, that she is a young lady now.

To escape the mother who is dependent and cruel at the same time, she marries the first man who asks. He is twice her age, and she is only fifteen. He is even worse than her mother and denies her custody of their baby daughter, thinking she won't dare leave.

She leaves him anyway. She is desperate.

Barely eighteen, she crosses the border. She's heard that dreams come true over there.

The years come and go. Another marriage, eight more children. At 70-years-old, my mother did not reach five feet tall, and there was nothing stooped about her. *Toda mi cara es una arruga*, my face is one humongous wrinkle, she would admit. But that's what two divorces, no chance at an education, smoking, coffee, sleepless days and nights of work, no money, and finally, drinking, will do to a woman who didn't know what the American dream would cost.

Mami has old-yolk fingernails from her years of restaurant-frying and disinfecting bed pans. Varicose veins clog her legs from the years of standing on the job.

A lightning bolt of gray streaks her naturally black hair, razored like a man's because she has more important things to worry about than beauty. High heels, anyway, because she has great legs, life is short, so let's go dancing.

Es un orgullo ser-mexicana. My mother began my Spanish classes as soon as I learned how to read in English. It is important to know two languages, she told me.

One day, you'll see. And year after year, the lessons continued. The Alamo? Santa Ana? He is a traitor. What are they teaching you in school? There is another side to everything. Remember that. Don't be ashamed of who you are.

Last June, then-presidential candidate George W. Bush made a fifteen-minute appearance before the National Association of Hispanic Journalists in Houston. We were asked to submit our questions in advance.

"Sir, if you were born poor, where would you be today?"

As someone read my words, I realized that poverty cannot be held in your head. You have to hold her in your arms, like my mother's.

Bush seemed surprised, but I think it was from nervousness. Rambled something about how he assumed he would have had good parents, and how he would have gone to college…he was sure. But he didn't seem sure at all.

My mother Marina never told me how she crossed the

border. Only that she was eighteen, and that she had big dreams.

Last year on October 7th, she died. Just a couple of days after Cuco Sánchez, the Mexican singer and composer, her favorite. I think she planned it.

"Don't forget me," she would write me, her first-born in the U.S. "When I'm gone, don't forget your brother in prison, the one who is disabled, reach out to the sister who has forgotten where she comes from. Don't let your baby brother get all squash-headed from his doctorate, visit your older sister in Mexico, she will need you more than ever. Be a *familia*, for once.

"Forgive each other for the past. Help each other. Love each other."

She made me promise.

"And don't forget the *mariachis* at my funeral. I don't care if you get me a cardboard casket. But don't forget my music."

She wanted trumpets, guitars, silver buttons blazing from their *charro* suits. "Have them sing '*La Barca de Oro*' when they drop me into the ground. Because at the next border, I have the right kind of papers. *Por favor, mijita,* don't forget."

She made me promise.

A Confession/The Priest

San Antonio Express-News • *June 17, 2002*

"My brother was raped by a priest. Can you help me?"

Dalia Garza, a *mujer decente* who I will find out is sixty but looks younger, is telling me a story that is more like a confession that God wants to make to the rest of us.

"I want the world to know," she says with the nothing-left-to-lose eyes of those women I met in Guatemala who had survived the civil war. And though I am busy and tired with my deadlines here in San Antonio, somehow a voice tells me to listen, because the stories that really matter are the ones that you have been searching for, but in all the wrong places.

As a former social worker, I have listened to my share of sexually abused and love-deprived children. But Dalia tells me a story so nightmarish that I called her therapist to verify her emotional state. Was she hysterical? Surely I had heard it wrong, though my instincts were telling me that this woman was not mad, but suffering deeply. No, she was suffering post-traumatic stress, said the therapist. She wasn't insane at all. She was furious, grieving with suppressed memories, and most of all—betrayed.

Because Dalia has seen the face of God, but he is not in the Church.

A child of the forties, Dalia's childhood was the ashes of the ashes of Frank McCourt's immigrant story set in San Antonio. Only she had the drunken father, Cayo, who forgot to sing the patriotic songs to Mexico and instead battered his wife, deliberately ran over his 18-month-old daughter—killing her (the newspaper reported it as an accident), raped and sodomized his children.

Dalia's memories are of 97 Flann Alley on the Westside, in a shanty that doesn't exist anymore where she and her family of five siblings starved. Of the living children then, Albert was the second oldest, and favorite brother to Dalia, who was just twenty months younger.

When Albert was six or seven years old, my father was threatening to kill him. My mother went to the church and asked for sanctuary. The priest sent her away, he said she had married in the church, she needed to stay in the marriage. I recall watching a neighbor trying to trap pigeons to feed his family. And the church did nothing, they had masses and catechisms, collected our pennies and nickels, charged us for baptism, marriages, funerals, etc., and instead of saving souls they destroyed our souls and watched, she wrote in her journal that she gave me after we talked.

Still, the family had faith.

Like my own brother once did.

Ox-eyes. That's what my mother called Jorge, because he was the only one of my seven brothers and sisters with the eyes that were different, and for that, envied. Brown-sugar eyes with long lashes that absorbed books day and night, trailed the baby rattlesnakes in the cotton fields where we worked, eyes more like torches, beacons, brown pools of a childhood that reflected bicycles, baby rabbits, poetry and mischief too. Jorge. My beloved *hermanito*, the oldest boy, the preferred son, my mother's dream-child, the chosen one destined to be handsome and gifted. And he is.

Now he's in prison where he's been most of his life. I have never understood the why of it—forgiven him the addictions to marijuana, heroin and cocaine. The robberies committed in the name of drugs. Most of all, I could not understand why he burned that money when he was twelve years old. In a night full of police and my father's disowning, a night of a fire started in a trash can whose flames have extinguished our whole family with its heat.

Like Jorge, Dalia's brother, Albert, was also an "A" student. But he had to run away as his father's threats, abuse and name-calling continued. Though he always returned. My father was not like Dalia's at all. He believed that a man must be a good father, and his children in turn must obey the father. Good boys don't cry, he taught us. If they want to be men.

Joto, queer, fag…my mother went to the church, spoke to the priest at Sacred Heart, 2123 W. Commerce, where we went to mass. The priest told my mother that she had married in the church, she must stay with my father and pray, he would pray also… My mother continued to pray. She would pray day and night for God to take my father away. She did pray for his death, she didn't pray for divorce. I guess because the church said that is a sin.

Finally, her prayers were answered. Dalia's father abandoned them and died a few years later in 1959. Overwrought with work and pain, Dalia's mother would eventually succumb to alcoholism and abuse too.

They moved from one relative to another…rats, roaches and bed bugs. *My mother was very sick, could hardly walk, she kept bleeding on and off, was anemic, and very poor nutrition…he and I were always together, we stuck together…*

Albert and Dalia, just one year apart, "were like fleas trying to survive in a hurricane," she tells me.

Desperate, Dalia's mother sent her to ask for charity…"I remember, walking, crying, and a big white fat priest came. What do you want? He yelled and screamed at me. What do you people think? That the Church can feed all of you?"

When I ask Dalia for his name, she answers that they didn't have names, they were just "Father." And that's why she hates the priests, because they all represent the one, and where was he when she needed him most? Isn't God mercy? Isn't God love? They take our nickles and dimes, she remembers. They have plenty of food, cars, a nice place to live.

And now I am also remembering how I learned in my church that we are all sinners, and the proof was that no matter how hard we tried, we never had anything. But God forgives, he sent his only son to wash away our sins, and the suffering today doesn't matter, there is paradise in heaven if we just wait, you'll see. Try to be like him, and obey, don't question him. The son is perfect, you see, not like your brother or my brother at all. And hating my brother is like hating myself, except the priests.

Then Albert went at age 12 to his Father (since he didn't have one) to ask the priest for help…to confide in him that he might be gay…and the priest raped him.

"Aren't they holy men?" Dalia says it is like being betrayed by God himself.

Albert was never the same again. He became addicted to heroin that same year, and didn't confide to Dalia about what happened at the Immaculate Heart of Mary until much later. Her brother was never able to break the habit which shadowed him all his life, and finally died of a brain hemorrhage, alone in his apartment at the age of 54.

Dalia hates the Church, and for a long time I did too. As women, we have seen that a male-dominated Catholic Church cannot teach us to be just or fair, because it is about men having power over women. Why else do they exclude us? Ultimately, they are the same as the men outside the Church, who seek to have power over other men, nations, tribes, the world. But they are not the son of God, but of women, aren't they?

"For this reason, our father, our brothers and sons are

less likely to talk about rape," says Norma Jean James, Dalia's therapist (LMSW, ACP). What follows, she says, is that many think they are homosexual. They are supposed to be the ones in power, in control, and what happens to their psyche when they learn how vulnerable they are? "Men have very fragile images of their sexuality," she says. "And they suffer from rape even more than women." The eloquent Ms. James reminds me of the sensitivity of her client case load. But when are women going to speak out on what they know to be true? Isn't the silencing of Dalia and her brother even worse than the abuse itself?

And as if she's reading my thoughts, James sighs. "We women at least talk to each other about our feelings…but men are not supposed to express themselves in this way."

There are good priests, she emphasizes. But the Church needs to change. Men are "wired for sex," and while women need sex as much as men, they can live without it if they have to. But men have a much harder time. "Studies have shown that men think of sex more," she says, and "the Church has become a shelter for sexually dysfunctional men.

"But don't confuse homosexuality with pedophilia," says the psychotherapist. "Homosexuality is not an aberration… we don't consider [it] a mental disorder, just another form of sexuality. The sexual violation of a child, pedophilia, is altogether a different thing," says James, carefully making a distinction that many confuse in their prejudice against lesbians and gays. "Pedophiles cannot be cured. I think that there's not an awareness that [pedophiles] are liars—they can beat the lie detector… There is never just one victim," she seems to have been waiting a long time to say this, but "hundreds and hundreds." And she answers my next question before I can ask it.

"Pedophilia seems to be with us since the beginnings of our male-oriented culture."

James feels that if women were priests, there would be less of this going on. Rome and Greece thought of it as an acceptable practice, she reminds me. Pre-adolescent boys were used as sexual consorts, and this may be our legacy of conquest and power. And then she says something that women intuitively understand in watching how the sons imitate the fathers: "Pedophiles have been sexually abused themselves." They never stop wanting to have sex with children, James underlines. "These people know they're going to have access—free access to young children…[in the Church]."

Unfortunately, mental health awareness has only become available in minority communities since the '80s. It is likely, the therapist agrees, that boys self-medicated themselves with whatever drugs they could find: heroin, marijuana, crack, cocaine, depending on the decade and availability.

Constance Hayes, 48, a licensed counselor for Adult Probation in Comal County, sees the correlation between drugs and sexual abuse every day. There is a "behavior change overnight…we have a picture of a boy carrying a cross," and the next thing you see is a picture of "him behind bars." Why? Then she tells me a shocking story that is not anymore.

Hayes' own brother, Jerry, was raped by a priest at the San José Mission Church in the fifties. Now lost to the family, Jerry wrote her a letter while he was in prison telling his favorite sister the whole story. He went from being an altar boy to being in detention, and like her colleague Dalia, she couldn't understand what changed him. Her family, she says, is still closed-mouth about it.

The irony of it all, says the embittered sister, is that in her work when sex offenders get probation, they are not allowed to explore sexuality. "They have to continually talk about how they victimized," not how they were victimized. It is only in the drug and alcohol program that the sexual abuse roots of their addiction are confessed.

Who was my brother?

Wanted to be a doctor.

Was a great dancer.

Was sensitive, took care of my mother and me, loved animals, played doctor all the time, mixed herbs to get color water and placed in bottles, did surgeries on my dolls, played soldier, cowboys and Indians, in school got good grades, was polite, got good grades in behavior, was creative, liked to draw, dance, could learn any dance steps. People would gather round to watch him dance. Was an actor, [indecipherable] a clown, etc. Loved to play at and make us laugh.

Had girlfriends.

As a reverent church-going family, my younger brother, Jorge, was under the tutelage of a charming Baptist youth minister back in the sixties. Then, suddenly, one summer night when he was twelve years old, he committed a mysterious act. Jorge burned the money he had stolen from the church.

I remember the flames rising from that trash can late that Sunday night, wondering why the whole backyard seemed to be on fire. Then I saw my little brother standing there. A skinny shadow trembling, inflamed with secrets that took me too long to understand. And though he has never told me, I forgive him for not crying.

I can still see his eyes, ox-eyes round and burning with the God in him. To me, he was perfect.

[My brother Jorge was never arrested for drug possession

or drug use. He told me that he has 12 first-degree convictions for Aggravated Robbery and one for Burglary. He's
been out of prison for 8 years.]

DRUGS IN THE FAMILY

Pacific News Service • Nov 24, 1997

Some of my best friends are drug dealers. One of them, Miguel Luís, [for the purpose of this article, I fictionalized all of the names] was the Chicano *"capo"* who handled business for the now-jailed García Ábrego clan. Its network stretched from Brownsville, Texas, to New York City—talk about making it!—and he was even featured in Hispanic Business 500.

The only time I read about him was when he was going to testify about the relationship between his boss and Raúl Salinas, the notorious brother of Mexico's former president.

Don't be shocked. Drugs have defined my family's struggle for the American dream. My brother, Gabo, is in a Texas prison for a series of armed robberies prompted by his cocaine addiction. My younger brother, David, died in 1993 from strep throat complicated by his long-time drug habits. You should have seen the funeral—a hundred grieving customers, from students to professors. It turns out he had sold nickel bags and pills for years to pay his University of Texas tuition. My sister Magda has detoxed from an affair with heroin.

It's easy to say that drugs are bad. But the people I know in the business, seller or users, are good. They're just trying to make it "the American way." But they figure the dream has a double standard—I have to play by the rules, you get to make them. They say the drug business is more honest than any corporation. "Look at pharmaceuticals, tobacco, the Ford Pinto case," says my friend Juan Antonio, the law student. "They know people have died using their products, and they don't care. In the narcoindustry, no one lies to you."

And unlike the rest of American business, the drug trade values Latinos. Bilingual and bicultural skills are critical for communications with Colombian and Mexican drug lords, and the intact family unit is essential for survival.

Yes, the risks are great, but the rewards are a dream come true. Latinos have grown up seeing the glamorous life on TV, just like everyone else, and drugs are the obvious route. Just say yes. Maybe you can't be a doctor—I never met a Latino physician until I was 30—but you can make more money than they do.

Miguel Luís may have dropped out of school, but that doesn't mean he wasn't ambitious. I suspect some of our best minds are laundering money because they were bored in school. With *"las drogas"* you can pioneer accounting and finance techniques faster than you can say FBI. You have to.

If it sounds like I'm proud of Miguel Luís—I am, in a way. What is the difference, anyway, between the *narco*-CEOs and the barons of the last century? Miguel Luís is the classic poor boy who made it. In a hundred years no one will ask how he became so rich.

I don't want to give you the impression that we're the bad guys because the drug culture that I know includes every-one. All in the same *familia*. My high school chum Adelina prosecutes people like my brother, whom she adored. Sal, the judge who could put Miguel Luís away for life, was a close friend of my late father-in-law. My friend Paulina, with her MD from Harvard, swears she could have saved my brother David because she knows—her own brothers have been ruined by drugs.

Next time you're in a room of professional Latinos, ask how many have a relative in prison for drugs? Wait for the denials. Then slowly, but surely, you'll hear, yes, a cousin once-removed is doing time for a robbery, he needed money for his fix. Then someone will talk about Tío Roberto whose car panels were stuffed with little plastic *bolsitas* of white powder. And the neighbor's grandson is using her house to sell homemade amphetamines. We've lived with these secrets for so long we don't think about them anymore. They're embarrassing. They confuse us.

My intimacy with the drug world has reminded me of something very important. That we are all connected to each other, even when we would rather forget it. If you're going to sell drugs, you need someone to buy them. There is Miguel Luís the drug lord and there is my brother Gabo the addict. One simply cannot live without the other.

The drug culture is a microcosm of haves and have-nots. It is America played out around my mother's kitchen table. For Latinos like me, the questions bite, the answers elude us. "Do something."

Why me? Because I am in the middle, the witness to this spectacle. I know the drug pusher, I went to school with the users. I go to receptions with the merchants who sell the Mercedes and Rolex watches that Miguel Luís bought. I know that whole economies would wither without the drug trade. I also know the drug war is not supposed to be won—because we want our drugs at any cost, and Latinos are going to pay that cost.

I am supposed to tell the truth. About playing ball with Henry, now in jail for burglary. Playing "makeup" with Zenaida, now a coke-head. Fishing with Toñio who is now a drug boss. These are our uncles, our cousins, the black sheep. We are the cops and the robbers, the bankers and the drug lords, and the line separating us is surprisingly thin. Believe me, a graduate degree doesn't mean much when your brother is in prison or dead.

Yes, the individual chooses. But society has never asked

me how to make that choice. Why I get to win when so many others have lost.

People say, "But you're different. You made it."

We think, "Sure. If you only knew."

Well, now you know.

THE LAND OF BARBACOA

Cornbread Nation UNC Press • 2005

Daddy dreamin 'bout it all the time.

When he isn't talkin about the war and all those dirty Japs he killed in the jungle. "Three years…you know how long that is? *¡No, vieja, no quiero arroz!* Slanty-eyed…"

Daddy won't touch my mother's *cilantro* rice. "Jap-food." Strictly a meat and potatoes man. Vegetables a dirty word to him, "are you kidding?" Slab of lettuce, a thick slice of fresh tomato, hand-picked from the *rancho* he worked as a sharecropper in the Texas Panhandle. A cool chunk of one of his fat cucumbers, maybe, but "don't forget the Thousand Island, *vieja!* Hot damn! Now that was a salad, told you we know how to eat in Texas!"

My father's family has always been here. "How long?" I ask Daddy, not telling him about the White kids in first grade who are chasing me, yelling at me to go back to Mexico. And the crying later. "Forever, I reckon." Daddy's proud our people settled Texas in the 1700s, and "then those thieving King Ranch people stole our land!" After the U.S.-Mexican War, he means. Never talks about the lynching and the way his grandfather was killed, but my mother says it's why Daddy's so mean sometimes.

That's how my father became a sharecropper working in the Panhandle, on this side of Oklahoma. No land left, you see.

People say he looks like one of those spaghetti-thin cowboys from the movies, a rougher Clark Gable-type with a sleepy voice like Nat King Cole's. *"¿Verdad que parece negro, comadre?"* Only Daddy speaks Spanish and English so well he doesn't need translation—all one song to him.

Daddy's grandfather had been a real cowboy. "Had to, no place to go—remember the Alamo?" "How can we forget, *por amor de Dios*, we lost!" *dice* Mami. Without land, the men went to work on the cattle drives—from their homes on the Texas border, all the way to the Canadian. Six months to get to Chicago with God's help, before the snowstorms hit.

When Daddy's talking like this, the Tejano in him plucks a guitar from somewhere out of the summer's blue sky, his baritone voice exploding with a song in the cotton fields surrounding us, making us see the cowboys beside him, right here on this land, singing their *corridos* with dust in their throats. Burning despite the snow.

Cuando salimos de Kiansas
con la fuerte novillada
ay que trabajo pasamos

"Damned hard work…not like the movies! What they don't tell you is that *mexicanos* were real cowboys, not like the *gringos.*"

My mother's really tired of his stories. Her family lost their land too, but in the Mexican Revolution. "Wasn't ours to begin with, the land belongs to everyone! That's what Zapata said, and what does your father think happens to those who steal it anyway? *¡Cabrones!*" Mami's in the kitchen, and she calls Daddy names under her breath 'cause he lets the *gringos* make him say *jes-sir!* and *no-sir!* and she wants him to be like Zapata and stand up.

My mother is *pura mexicana*. "Don't forget, head to toe!" She's not even five feet tall and though at twelve I'm already bigger than her, she still uses the belt on me. *¡Hijos de María Morales!* But Daddy's six feet tall and he laughs at my mother's smallness, her poetic bullets whizzing by, her politics for sure.

"You had to cross that border to eat, didn't you?"

Mami says that Mexico is paradise and that Texas is *puro* hell. *¡Un pinche infierno!* She says that over there across the river, there are mountains and volcanoes, orchids, chocolate and dancing at the *plaza* on Sundays. Explains that Mexico's problem is she's like a beautiful woman who everyone wants to possess. Like land. But nobody can have her, she doesn't belong to men.

I don't understand this, but Mami sure doesn't let Daddy boss her around.

She wants him to leave the *rancho* and get a real job in town. But Daddy's expecting a good harvest this year, making up for all the bad years before. I already know this because I heard them arguing late into the night about all the money they're owing for school clothes, for my brand-new flute and the sewing machine from Sears that Mami wanted so she could help Daddy pay the bills.

Then the harvest finally, really, comes. Daddy's humming Hank Williams, pinching Mami's *nalgas* when he thinks nobody sees. We're going to the town barbeque! With all the big *gringo* ranchers and everything! Daddy himself slaughters a cow so that there's gonna be plenty of good *comida*. Everybody smackin their lips, because the barbeque out-smells the cotton gin any day. Better than Christmas with those chilibeans, mashed potatoes and cole slaw, peach cobbler and buckets of iced tea. Daddy's harvest. And of course, miles of barbeque extending like rich, jagged acres of brown-sauced dreams.

Daddy remembers the way his family used to cook their meat in a special pit in the ground lined with stones and *mesquite* wood. Now that was a party! *¡Bautismos!* Birthdays! Easter! Welcome home! Slow-cooking a whole cow's head until, after several days, "it would melt in your mouth and make you forget all your *penas*!" Those *barbacoa* days with

his family kept him alive during the worst days of the Big
War, he said. Reminds us that the cowboy's barbeque comes
from the *vaquero* tradition. How it was the sweet and spicy
dribbling from the handmade corn *tortillas* all the way down
to the elbows at his grandfather's wedding *fiesta. Las manchas*
on his French great-grandmother's linens with the red *chile
salsa* before that and sticking to the fringes of his great-great
grandmother's *rebozo* way before her.

"Who cares if I didn't get a Purple Heart?" This *barbacoa*
proves he's a good man after all. Even if he doesn't have land
anymore.

But the boss man steals his harvest anyway. Mami and
Daddy divorce a few years later, and I never had *barbacoa*
again.

Until I moved to San Antonio. And here, every Sunday
morning, there are lines of cars outside places like Adelita's
and Big Joe's. The kids are waiting at home and they've placed
their order early with *Apá* for *pura carne*, and they've never
seen a whole *cabeza* bundled with *maguey* leaves in the
ground, but they know what they like with their breakfast.
Corn *tortillas, Papá!* Flour! *¡Salsa! ¡Gorditas!* Refried beans!
¡Papitas! Scrambled eggs! Sunny-side up! *¡Pico de gallo!* Avo-
cado! Juice! Coffee! A cold bottle of Big Red! Please, Daddy!
¡Por favor, Papi!

And all over *San Anto*, families gather 'round the table
as the father brings home a carton of just beef, or just cow's
head, after getting up extra early to be in line at six on Sunday morning. That's what a good father does.

And the hot meat is silky and juicy and *ay,* how good it
tastes, how the kids are laughing and the grease delicious,
like memories slipping from the mouth to the chin to the
table. Staining us with the past. Like blood. Like the land.

Just like it did that summer when we were a family.

IV.
MEXICO AND
CHILE
(THE COUNTRY)

ALL SHE WANTED WAS A KISS

*After "Enamoramiento," a sculpture
by José Luís Rivera at the San Antonio Museum of Art*

The color of chocolate-roses, the smell of comino
shaking from the roots after the dam-breaking rains
The ringing of bells on Christmas day the pianissimo
of tears

She searched day and night for the perfumed, fantastical,
smoke that comes before and after
  the dancing
A barefooted sock-hop, a Saturday-night disco,
Motown in the wet sand, street-tango in Chile,
a Cuban rumba on the malecón, gypsies
  in Granada
The squeezed ribs of Lerma's polkitas.

It was not enough.

She found it in the trash. In the fresh papers of
indocumentados salvaged from tú-no-importas countries,
breathless railroad cars and machine-guns lining them up,
words in a bad poem like this. She found it in the red-ink
dripping, praying, for a story.

She finds a muddy kitten, soquete instead of milk
in her throat sees a cardboard-man rising
from the gutter, hears the word: Puta.
The seven-year-old girl forced to dance
for her father and his friends. The eight-year-old boy
shamed for daring to look at another.

For one kiss, she is a starving dog, waiting forever
for a kiss like that, borrachos drink at the cantinas
on Zarzamora, others surrender to strawberry ice cream,
pizza and late-night nachos at Mi Tierra.
For one volcanic kiss, she embraces the impossible:
the tsunami, the big earthquake, a New Orleans
hurricane, the execution of innocents
and the rescue of mineros from Chile from the
tail of the world.

For one kiss like this, she forgives everything,
welcomes the breaking heart of *Enamoramiento.*
For the miracle of mesquite, the besotted
sculptor carves a kiss from wood
from a land that isn't even his anymore.

PASS THE SALSA
AND LA CONCIENCIA

Los Angeles Times • Sep 20, 1998

Mexican. A word that depends. Sometimes people spit it out, like they did in school, when the word was spiked with all the hate I could possibly carry on my first-grade back. It was a word my Tejano father denied as his heritage. To my mother, the word was delicate as *jacaranda,* perfumed with stories, immense as the *lapis lazuli* sky of Mexico, where she's from.

Like the story of the U.S.-Mexican War, a PBS production aired nationally last week, the words depend on who is telling the story. You see, the U.S.-Mexican War is my becoming, a Mexican-American who calls herself a Latina, a Chicana, because my story begins with this war. My family as descendants of the Cavazos land grant in Texas, resided between the disputed boundaries of the Nueces and the Río Grande rivers that served as the excuse for the war. As a result of the U.S. victory, my ancestors became Americans overnight—and ultimately lost about a million acres now encompassed by the famous King Ranch.

I'm glad I don't have any land left. Though my father has grieved all his life, and clings to the one scrap of land remaining as proof that we were something once, that we belonged. That proof is a family cemetery in San Perlita, a town known as a little pearl that reminds me of the Magi's lesson of the price we pay for wealth.

No, if I had some land, then I would think I'm better than someone who doesn't. I'm not. My Spanish ancestors claimed the land from my Indian grandmothers. After the

U.S.-Mexican War, my father's Cajun side came to Texas and married the rest of it through a union with a *mestiza* from South Texas whose family had always been here. Now, my land is my language—an amalgam of English and Spanish, the disputed territory of Tex-Mex and Spanglish, the *Caló* that embarrasses people like my mother, and all the words I absorb from the rich dialects of Blacks and immigrants I meet.

I'm in the middle of this war because I'm an American by birthright, and a Mexican by heartright, though neither side accepts me as the human legacy of this war. All my life, I have been told that my English is really good, considering I was born in Mexico. My Mexican relatives call me a *gringa* who doesn't speak her Spanish like a native. It took me a long time to realize wars are resolved by meeting in the middle. I embody a war from which all the others revolve, with its mutual lessons of conqueror and conquered, each side hungering for what the other seems to have, while we deny the best of each. It is my destiny, then, to be a witness to the war that has no end in sight.

But I don't think we want to resolve this war. There are no Chicanos in the creative production of the U.S.-Mexican War, except for one. That's because neither side wants to share the land, and meet in the place where I reside. The *Americanos* devour *tacos* and the Mexicans devour English—but neither recognizes me, because we are afraid of the middle ground. Of the America we might become.

Neither side wants to become something new, something different, because that would be inferior to who they imagine they are. There is too much at stake, a journey we don't want to make, even when we know there is more to this, as we warily eye each other across the river amid barbed wire and *abrazos*.

Yet, the resolution is in that borderland where I live. That is the place in the disputed territory that provided the excuse for the war. I am that middle which has seen the masculine imperative that demands war, the racism seeping from both sides, the pretensions of class from all angles, the profiles of feminism and sexuality that dissolve into the other like the streams that flow into the Río Grande. I have seen this because I cross borders every day, and I am telling you there is another world to discover.

In Guanajuato, México, where I lived, the upper class was confounded by my casual brown presence in the coffee shops along with my laptop—an emblem of status there. But they were more confused by my friendliness with the waiters who look just like me. The middle class envied my English but rarely my concern for civil rights. They have no experience with the ideals of democracy, only the ideals of class. The Harvard-bred leaders of Mexico don't recognize equality, they've never lived it and will never pay my relatives a decent wage. They want to be like the United States in our consumption, not the consuming of democracy, *nomás fíjate* the assault on Chiapas—the Wounded Knee of Mexico. Mexico, like the United States, glorifies her Indian heritage as she does everything possible to destroy her flesh-and-blood Indians.

The U.S.-Mexican War rages, and people like me, the Latinos, Chicanos, are the borderline between the victory or defeat of our humanity toward each other. Every illegal immigrant who crosses could be my mother 40 years later. My youngest brother is getting a Ph.D. What did the new settlers of the Southwest think they would create by teaching their children to call me names at school and treat me as a token at work? What did the rich Mexicans imagine, that their children would not have to face someone like me one day, the child of one of their nobody *campesinos,* a child of the Civil Rights Movement, a grandchild of one of those revolutionary peons, across the table at the White House?

Words. We, as the bastard children of this war, are the ones who can interpret this war so we can understand each other. We know the meaning of the words behind the words, how the war continues on the cultural, social and economic fronts. This is a war without bullets, yet far more violent because we cannot see or touch it. No bloodless documentary can heal the wounds that are beyond words that can't be translated, the words that must be confronted, one by one, if we are to find the peace that we ask the rest of the world to find.

I don't know if we have the courage to find that world. It requires that we meet in the center, and that's a place more substantial than *chipotle* and Cheerios. It means you will have to travel farther than Cancún or Disneyland. You will come to the middle, to the disputed territory, to confront what you have done, and apologize. It means that you trust there is another America, the kind that includes me, not as symbol, but in practice. That this land was never meant to be yours, or even Mexico's. That it, like me, is a symbol of the possible. That you have many borders to cross, that you are not afraid, that you will never be the same again.

Then the war will finally be over.

BLAMING THE IMMIGRANT/ GUANAJUATO, GTO., MÉXICO

San Antonio Express-News • *1996*

The *señora* is begging for money again. She is hungry. Just like Mexico.

Every day that I pass her on the way to my favorite *taquería,* she sits on the same corner, her three children crouched in little shadows, asking for a few *centavos.* This woman, Josefina, is embarrassed when I ask her why she is suffering. Her husband has died, she explains. There is no one to help with the plot of land, there isn't enough to eat. She is skinny. The dirt glitters on her like quartz. Her children look like they have parasites.

But the shopping is *sooooo* good. I overhear the tourists, mostly my *gringo paisanos* from the U.S., talk about the bargains they just got on the Talavera ceramics, the wool *sarapes* from Saltillo, the silver jewelry from Taxco. Mexico, after all, is synonymous with cheap.

There is a reason we flock to Cancún or Mexico City for our vacations. Or cross the border to get a beer and a haircut. This country is a bargain basement of delights. The American middle class can feel—is—absolutely rich here. Mexico is like buying the most beautiful prostitute of our dreams for the price of an old whore. Tempting, hypnotic, erotic. No wonder Uncle Sam likes to visit. *¡Viva México!*

And the United States? If only they would get out of here, then everything would get better. So America could be a utopia again. Ronald Reagan country, when we were safe and everybody went to church. It doesn't matter that most Mexicans are socially conservative and go to mass every

Sunday. It's the new world order that is scaring everybody, the globalization of markets and peoples affected by those job currents. May the force be with us…because the free enterprise system that we have worshipped for so long does not worship us.

It's not the immigrants we should blame, but ourselves.

The United States is rich because Mexico is poor. It's not just our fault. The Mexican elite have been silent partners in the deal too. But the very exploitation of Mexico and the rest of Latin America that fueled the Industrial Revolution and our modern standard of living is now exploiting us—with the monsters we created. These are the multinational corporations, and they scour the Earth looking for low-wage labor in third-world countries.

In the name of profit, we forgive our corporations for the kinds of sins that we would never commit. Consorting with tyrants. Ecological disasters. Abuse of human rights. Slave labor. And all of this is happening with our blessings, because our Puritan ethic tells us that money means we are good, no matter what we've done to earn it.

Don't slam the door behind you. While we're beating up on immigrants, the companies are beating on us even worse. More than 600,000 people are now employed in the *maquiladoras*, most, American-owned, that take advantage of cheap Mexican labor. And cheap is the word. In January, Guess announced that it would concentrate all its production in Mexico. A textile worker there makes $1.08/hour compared to the U.S. standard of $7.08. Believe me, that's not real money in Mexico where it takes $16 a day to feed a family.

Union organizers have been met with resistance, firings, and violence from police in the thrall of big business. Corporate investments are largely short-term for infrastructure, equipment and labor. And these corporations pay little or no income tax as part of their incentive for coming south. In other words, Mexico is not getting rich because of NAFTA, but the companies sure are.

There is a reason we have free-trade agreements that don't include the free movement of people. The deal goes like this: We sell you technology and junk, you sell us precious minerals and a culture that is thousands of years old. Our addicts get their drugs, and you get decertified. You do something about the Zapatistas so that we can feel secure about our investments in your lands, while you buy more cars without catalytic converters to make your own pollution.

When your peasants can't compete with agribusiness, we'll sell you Wonder Bread *tortillas*. Last year, Mexico lost 250,000 jobs when she imported 5 million tons of maize.

Poverty depends.

If one is poor and there is a reason to dream, it can give a person depth, stamina, character. But when there is no perceptible hope of changing your life, it can destroy the soul. Mexico is heart-rending poverty. Two-thirds of Mexicans are unemployed or make less than $10 a day. According to the government's own statistics, 14 million people, or 15% of the nation, live in absolute misery.

The middle class is difficult to stabilize. The *peso* devaluation wrecked it far worse than the earthquake. But the 40% of the families between the lowest third and highest third account for 27% of the nation's wealth. This kind of middle class is just holding on by its *uñas*.

If Mexico was known as a country of extremes before, it is a case-study of a polarized *mundo*. The top 10% have almost 40% of the nation's income. And up until the famous "crisis" in 1994, Mexico had the distinction of having bred

30 billionaires—right behind the U.S. and Japan.

In Mexico, the poor lick the trash cans of the rich.

So what? That's their problem.

Thanks to our new immigration and welfare laws, it is now open season on the poor, the illegal, the ignorant, and the different. Make no mistake, it's an ideology that will bite you too—sooner or later. Because this war is about saving America, and no one I know has explained what that has to do with hating immigrants.

I suspect that the people who are in support of the hysteria are also against Blacks, gays, feminists, and other high-risks to our status quo. Tell me, what is an American, anyway? What exactly does he or she look like?

Speak English. As if we are too stupid to speak two or three languages at once. We have let our politicians turn us into patriotic fools. America: Love it or leave it. We confuse national identity with cultural hegemony.

Children of immigrants are in the White House, on Wall Street, playing basketball, or on network television. They have forgotten. But then our grandparents, *a la* Secretary of State Madeleine Albright, who recently discovered that she is Jewish, didn't want to remember how they got here, either.

No comment. For all of Mexico's protests, who certainly doesn't want the poor either, these *pobres* serve as a critical point of reference. You see, the Mexican elite is trying too hard to imitate *los gringos,* and the *ilegales* remind them of all that they are not.

I think it's Mexico's *destino* to be poor. We simply cannot afford for them to have what we take for granted because the world cannot tolerate the consumption. Think of the garbage, the pollution, the automobiles, the forests kindled, the petroleum burned, if they lived like we do. Just look at

Mexico City. But this is exactly the kind of progress we have given the world.

Perhaps we hate the immigrant so much because they are the embodiment of all that we have done to each other. A symbiotic past smeared with desire, envy, greed, repulsion. Dancing to the tune of fear. It is more difficult to love and it is so easy to hate. There might not be enough for all of us. A curse whispered during the ceremonial *abrazo*.

La señora is hungry still. But we are the real beggars of the world.

IMMIGRANTS HAVE A STORY TO TELL US

San Antonio Express-News • *June 18, 1995*

Every immigrant to this country has a different story to tell. And the more we resist knowing, the more they haunt us.

Recently, two new films—*Mi Familia/My Family,* and *The Pérez Family*—tell distinct versions of the immigrant's encounter with the American Dream.

In *Mi Familia,* the story is a Mexican one. It could be—is—like my own family. A symphony of *mariachis,* each one of the six children in the Sánchez family is unique because they are the necessary parts of the whole. The steadfast dream is one of family, despite what America has done for—and to—them. We see that one will prosper, and one will go to prison. One will save others, and one will die for his rebellion. One will deny his heritage, and one will honor with his story. This is the family we all belong to, but are afraid to see.

With the film *The Pérez Family,* however, the Cuban immigrant story is told as a sugarcane fantasy wrapped in desire. And in the representative body of the main character, Dorita, the American dream is a carnal one. She wants. Her dreams are nail polish, discos and swaggering men like John Wayne. Ultimately, she is redeemed by a family of new refugees like herself, all named Pérez, who have seen that the other side of a dream—if you aren't part of it—is a nightmare.

The films vividly show us that not all immigrants are the same and that the American Dream has always depended on who is doing the dreaming…

The Mexicans and the Cubans first arrived in large numbers following their respective revolutions. But the arrivals were on different sides of the war. The Mexican Revolution in 1910 was fought over land reform, and while it was a political revolution, it was never a social one.

The Cubans who came here in the early waves following their own revolution in 1959, also lost their lands—in the symbol of Fidel Castro. But their revolution was a social victory for the poor, and as a result, the rich *cubanos* came to America in search of their lost wealth.

The dream, then, for the Mexicans, is a spiritual one. The Mexican just wants to live after the revolution. The Cuban wants to live as he did before the revolution.

Both films should help us to dream with our eyes open. The Sánchez family and the Pérez family translate the American dream to make it their own reality. Their dream is either one of family, or one of prosperity. And the happy endings begin when they discover that one isn't worth much without the other.

We are fascinated with the immigrants because they are our past, and they have a story we can barely remember. We get as close to them as we dare. We learn Spanish, savor plates of fried *plátanos*, black beans, and *enchiladas*, discovering the *salsa*-queen Celia Cruz because we want to dance like we mean it.

But we are still not as brave as the immigrants.

Perhaps we are envious because they are on their journey, and we are almost finished with ours.

LA COLA DEL MUNDO, SANTIAGO DE CHILE

La Voz de Esperanza • Oct 2000

Here I am at the tail of the world, hanging on for dear life. *La cola del mundo,* as they say in Santiago de Chile. Buried my mother the day before I left San Antonio. She's the reason I made it here, to this place so far from home.

A place surrounded by Cool Whip mountains that are higher than the Rockies. Where our winter is their summer, and there is jasmine in November, like a dream I have had of a place that I've been to before, a dream more real because it feels like I never left.

¿De dónde es usted? Brazilian? Peruvian? Costa Rican? The *chilenos* can't figure out where I'm from. Curious, half-way between the Mexican never-met-a-stranger ways and the reticence mistaken for the uppityness of their Spanish ancestors, they look at me and wonder. You can't be from the United States, a local vendor tells me, shaking her head. You're not blonde and blue-eyed.

Too much American television, I laugh.

When they find out I was born in the USA, they are shocked. They have seen *los gringos* in Santiago, of course, along with the French, the Canadians, the Swiss, the British, the Dutch, the Japanese and German. Even the Scots. The hordes of evangelicals. But me? There is Jennifer López and *el* Michael Jordan. But me? Then I remind them of the U.S.-Mexican War, remember? And they nod, *¡claro, como no!* They don't say it. But I know that they are thinking about the conquest that brought them here. Then they tell me about their own conquest of land from Perú. They have realized how borders can change from one day to the next.

Pololo, poroles, vicuna, guaguas, callampas. Boyfriend, green beans, llama, shantytowns, children. Mapuches. The indigenous people of Chile. Their Spanish is not like mine, and they can't understand why I stumble trying to follow their bird-song chirping, a language sweet and salty at the same time. Like their *salones de té* with little fancy pastries a few hours after a seafood soup served with red *chile pebre*. The conversation begins with *hola* and finishes with *po'* instead of my *pues*, or the German *ja* instead of the *sí* that I'm used to. Not even the Mexican *sale* for *vale* here. But I like it anyway. The Chileans remind me of what children grow up to look like when we Latinos marry *gringos*. Stubborn black hair, lots of it, though the skin fades. But here and there you see copper-coated skin like mine. And it never fails to surprise, like the shadows that fall across the decaying colonial buildings at sunset.

Though they recognize their Mapuche heritage, the indigenous nation of Chile which is still fighting for their land, the *chilenos* are *chilenos*. *Chi-le-nos*, they tell me. To be distinguished from the *omnipotentes—los argentinos,* or the shorter and refugee-status Peruvians who crowd the city's cathedral on Sundays. We are racist, many admit. Blacks, who are maybe one percent of the population, are ugly. *La nariz apachurrada*, their noses flattened. And the rich don't want to share with the poor, the same noses wrinkle.

And take Pinochet back with you, *por favor*, we give him to you. After 16 years of dictatorship, the old general is a satire on their own version of *Saturday Night Live.* Where he dances with Margaret Thatcher as if they were lovers. The following Monday, the cell phones swarm along *Huérfanos*, the city's impressive Wall Street. On that redstone *esplanada*, you can hear the *tango's bandoneón* and the indigenous *quena* on the same block with the romantic *"Devuélvame la vida."* Then if you are a woman, you can only dream of getting a good coffee at the *salones* called Haití and Caribe. There, your espresso is dispensed by young women perched on stiletto heels wearing white spandex miniskirts so mini that their legs seem to fuse with the curved table where the men stand in droves for their—um—coffee. What would the *generalísimo* think, after so many years of curfews and moral preaching, I wonder?

We need a break, the Chileans tell me, and it is far more interesting to gossip about the latest installment of their own Argentine President Carlos Menem. Even if he is seventy years old and twice her age, Cecilia Bolocco, or *La Bolocco*, as she is commonly known, is a former Miss Universe (aren't they all in Latin America?), talk show host and ravishing blonde with a penchant for white ball gowns that reveal this-is-the-real-thing-*chichis*.

La Bolocco has been grabbing the headlines instead of another bombshell. Not Pinochet. Because he doesn't deserve the attention, my friends tell me.

THE EVANGELICALS, SANTIAGO DE CHILE

San Antonio Express-News • Nov 18, 2000

This city, which suffered a military dictatorship for sixteen
years, is suffused in the pink of poinsettia trees, ripe-orange
flamboyán, and a tree that sparkles with lavender. It's spring
here, and the Andean mountains that embrace this city still
have winter snow, creamy, like Duncan Hines.

Pedro de Valdivia, fresh from the conquest of Perú,
alongside Pizarro, arrived in the Mapocho Valley in 1541.
Today, the capital city of Santiago, which is James in English, is surrounded by invaders more treacherous than the
mountains. By the twin arches of McDonalds, the wonders
of the Sheraton Hotel, the faith in capitalism as the ultimate
answer.

And now, the evangelicals have arrived.

Twelve of them from the United States. Twelve, like the
apostles. The women who run my *residencial* on Catedral
Street in the center of Santiago are busy scrubbing, mopping
with *cloro*, waxing the once upper-crusty wooden staircase
in this almost two-hundred-year-old Spanish colonial man-
sion. Now a bohemian neighborhood filled with graffiti and
gutsy slogans telling Pinochet he is an assassin.

Inez, the prim and proper lady who works most nights,
tells me that she likes the evangelicals because they don't
stay up late at night. Like the rest of us travelers, she means.
They're so pure, she explains. Get up at six in the morning,
out by eight and go to sleep by nine. She likes to get her
sleep, you see, instead of getting up in the middle of the
night when the doorbell sings its music box chime. Though

we have keys to our rooms, Inez acts as the night watchman too, securing the heavy grillwork gate inside the doorway when the last one comes in.

Chichi, her retarded 30-year-old daughter, follows her around, a smaller shadow that mimics her sounds and sighs. And scolds when I come in late.

The next morning, the *evangélicos* take up the whole dining room and wake me up because my room faces the common area. Convenient most days, because I can just open my door in my *piyamas* and sit down for a typical breakfast of hard rolls, a slice of homemade apple pie, called *kuchen* here, a glass of imitation orange juice, and Nescafé.

Today is different. I hear the leader rally the troops once all the scraping and coffee cupping has stopped. Apparently they're here to build a house or something like that, and he seems to be giving a pep talk to the apostles who must be in a kind of culture shock.

"I know this is not what you expected," he begins to preach. "This is poorer than you're used to, but Jesus Christ would not have stayed at the Hilton…," he quotes some scripture and then somebody gives testimony, something about converting a doctor's wife after offering her husband a Bible to read. The leader says that he knows it's difficult to convert others when you don't know the language—apparently none of them speak Spanish.

When I walk into the dining room, they barely notice. Inez tells me later that she was surprised they didn't see I was American like them, and speak English to me. Have to explain how *gringos* don't see me as one of them, as I am to her. That I'm supposed to "speak English" in the United States, and with all of that, they have forgotten how much Spanish I still remember.

Don't know how to explain Americans and their fear

that bilingualism somehow will make people like me less American. How I may be a *gringa* to her, but not to the *gringo-gringos*.

After they leave, my buddies Stefan, the Scot, and Fabrice, *el francé*s, saunter in. I tease the men in Spanish that they are too late for the evangelicals, who neither wants to confront. "They scare me," Fabricio says. He has told me that Americans are fat, and eat food that is tampered with hormones. Though he's traveled in Africa, he's afraid to go to the United States. "You have guns. And George Bush."

Stefan, who is taller than Fabrice, skinny as the native araucaria trees here, and could pass for my darkest brother, asks me, "Why don't Americans know where they're from?" He says that one of the *evangélicos* asked him where he came from and when he answered Scotland, the man's eyes opened bloody wide and proceeded to tell him that his ancestors were from there too. You have to understand that Stefan's accent is full of bloody this and mum that, and he pronounces his birthplace as in *Scautlaund*. But where, exactly? The man didn't know, so Stefan asks me, "Why don't they know?"

"Why don't Americans know where they come from?" he repeats. "Why don't the evangelicals learn Spanish?" Fabrice complains. This angular, handsome *howdotheydoit* Frenchman, even when they don't take a bath, according to Gloria and Lina who arrive for the morning's shift, and are pestering me about this while the *francés* speaks in English to me. Or maybe I'm the only one who understands his Spanglish with all the *zee-ing* and *oui-ng*. "Why don't the Chileans speak better *inglés*?" this windsurfer questions in frustration. So many tourists here, he presses. He says that I'm not like the Americans he imagined.

"One question at a time, please." I tell Stefan that the

immigrants who left Europe left everything behind, including their memory. That's good, maybe, he muses. But it's
also bad, isn't it? Turning to Fabrice, I ask him why don't the
French speak better English, considering they have so many
tourists too? He laughs. "We're French." And then I tell
Gloria and Lina that I don't know why the Europeans don't
take baths as often as we do, but it must have something to
do with their ancient history of deprivations or revolutions,
or something.

"*Non.*" The Frenchman interrupts. "The water's too cold."
It seems he doesn't understand how to work the hot water
heater.

When I translate to Gloria and Lina how the evangelicals were shocked by the poverty of this *residencial*, they
don't understand. Striving for the right words, I translate
that most Americans aren't used to sharing bathrooms or
bedrooms, even in return for balconies, chandeliers, and the
eternal friendship of *los chilenos.* You are different, I explain.
And to be different, means to most of us, and to the evangelicals, that you must therefore be less equal.

"Fabrice, are you a *gringo* too?" Gloria asks, points to his
unwashed hair. "Because you look like one." "French," he
answers proudly. "Stefan?" "Scauttish." "*Y yo soy americana.*"
Then we begin to laugh.

We realize that the wars and invasions we represent took
our land, and more. They almost conquered our potential to
see each other as equals. Because there are borders inside us
that are so deep and dark they make climbing the Andean
mountains simple.

We are just not going to be what the evangelicals expect.

But, then, we are not what we expected either.

REGRESÉ DE MIS VIAJES: SEEKING PABLO NERUDA, ISLA NEGRA, CHILE

La Voz de Esperanza • 2001

But I haven't told you about Pablo Neruda and his three houses.

In Santiago, Isla Negra, and Valparaíso. The sixteen editions of *Robinson Crusoe*, the butterflies, the driftwood that became his writing table. The inscription at the entrance to his ship-in-a-house at Isla Negra: *I returned from my travels. I sailed making happiness.*

A child of poverty, the Nobel prize-winning poet and political activist died within days of the military coup of 1973 which claimed the life of his close friend, Salvador Allende. Though the military ransacked his houses, his widow Matilde organized a foundation in his name. The poet had no heirs, and left everything to the people of Chile.

A couple of blocks down from Empanatodos, where you can get twenty-five varieties of the famous Chilean staple, in the bohemian-chic Bellavista, at the foot of the Cerro de San Cristóbal, is the poet's Santiago home. A nondescript sign, dangling from its post and marked with graffiti, simply says: *La Chascona, Fundación Pablo Neruda.* Unless you ask, you don't know you have to walk up the narrow street to your right that rises like a silent wave. Neruda named his house La Chascona in honor of his Matilde's unruly hair.

The house is a multi-stories ship on land, like all of his houses. Born near the water, Neruda loved the ocean, though he couldn't sail his own rowboat because he got seasick. That didn't stop him from adorning his homes with

a captain's table and heavy masculine chairs, always with
low roofs to simulate a voyage, fully-equipped bars and
little tables for drinking *pisco*. And, at Isla Negra, a museum
full of *proas*, the mythical female (and sometimes male or
animal) totems that guide the ship to safety.

There, the ocean is a constant murmur, like a lover's
sweet whisperings in your ear. It is a rocky coast, something
like California without the crashing waves. Once a simple
fishing village, Isla Negra is now filled with tour buses,
souvenir shops and a restaurant called Twenty Poems of
Love. Outside his house, the bells make their music from
the giant wind chime that he constructed, and there they
stand, a beacon for the traveler who has come home at last.
And never forgets where he came from.

Neruda collected everything. Masks from around the
world, rare insects under glass, pre-Incan statuary, and glass
bottles from Venice, hand-sculpted pipes for his tobacco
habit, Chilean paintings from his famous friends, English
china, Russian dolls, and African goddesses of fertility.
When he won the Nobel prize, he bought two sets of the
first edition of the French encyclopedia, and his book-
shelves display his favorite Dickens, Lord Byron, Whitman,
and Jules Verne. The visitor is allowed to almost touch
Neruda's books, and it is easy for me to read the titles of
his Latin American collection, which has books on ento-
mology, botany, history, the flora and fauna of the land that
these books confess he loved so deeply. In French, German,
English and Spanish.

I wish Neruda would have been with me the night before
because I needed his help, his words, to help me understand
the Chile I didn't want to know. And love despite.

But *el destino* has other plans as you well know, and that's
how I ended up dining at the *elegantísimo* home of Lucía

and Tabo. Recommended to me by Josie Negrete, who had
met Lucía, a fellow *profesora,* through the internet. Lucía is
a distinguished educator at the Universidad Católica, and
her husband, Tabo, is a banker. Lucía, so *rubia* that the *gringos* think she is one of them, gave me a tour of her exclusive
Las Condes suburb, pointing out the private schools that
her accomplished children have attended. She and Tabo, *"el
negro,"* are from the oldest and most prominent families of
Chile.

   Her family helped build Santiago, she proudly told me.
Later, I would read that the Spaniards arrived in Chile in
the mid-sixteenth century, led by Pedro de Valdivia, the
conquistador sent by Francisco Pizarro after the defeat of the
Incas in Perú. There is a grand statue to him on horseback
at the Plaza de Armas, the city's historical center. Valdivia
rewarded his followers with enormous land grants, some
stretching from the Andes to the Pacific. The *encomienda*
system, Spanish grants of huge land tracts and the rights
to Indian labor and tribute, has been an enduring fixture
of Chilean history and politics, given its isolation. Maybe,
I wonder, is that the reason that Chile's politics have been
so violent? Is the class system that intractable? But I don't
say anything to Lucía. Anyway, I can't say in Spanish what I
have learned first in English.

   Valdivia died at the battle of Tucapel in 1553, at the
hands of the famous Mapuche *caciques* Caupolicán and
Lautaro. In the same *plaza*, across the way from Valdivia's
prominence, there is an abstract monument to the
Mapuches—a post-modern tribute of a fragmented face.

   Lucía and Tabo's home is filled with native *artesanía*
and artifacts from Rapa Nui, a result of a daughter's visit to
Easter Island, a Polynesian colony of Chile. "Speak English
to her," asks Lucía of her college-age daughter, when she

arrives as we're talking in the garden, besides the altar to *La Virgen de Lourdes*. Like most Latin Americans these days, they marvel at my command of English, and make great sacrifices for their children to be fully bilingual. While I marvel at their turquoise swimming pool, and they tell me they have another one at their second home by the beach. The maid is a young *peruana* who wears a uniform and is quiet and brown like me. She is one of three servants who Lucía employs, not counting the help for the beach house. As Lucía begins to detail her charitable hiring of the *peruana*, who showed up desperate at her door one day, a refugee of the Peruvian economy, her daughter is embarrassed. "Shshshshshsh, *mamá,* can't you see that she will hear us?" As if she senses the maid might be hurt by Lucía's *noblesse oblige.*

Then we sit down for a late-night feast of crab salad, filet mignon, chardonnay and a fruit meringue dessert with espresso. I explain that my mother is Mexican, but that I grew up in the United States, and that's why my English is so good, *que me atoro con el español.* None of them have been to the U.S. before, though they've been to Europe many times, and to the blue ice-land of Tierra del Fuego. I can tell that Lucía and Tabo are struggling to understand, that they have never met someone like me before. We talk about NAFTA, our educational system, San Francisco, Washington D.C., good wines and Mexico. They are very curious about Mexico especially. They must visit, Mexico is so *fantástico.* We talk about the indigenous cultures of Mexico, and I tell them what little I know: the pyramids, the *mantelería*, toy airplanes made from Coca-Cola cans, *flan de mango.* And how we Mexicans are like the seven types of *mole.* Somehow this takes us to the subject of land, the Zapatistas, the Mexican Revolution, and the status of

Chicanos like me in the U.S.

My hosts want to know, but are afraid to know at the same time. I can tell. They want to be cosmopolitan, but are smart enough to not ask me about the struggle that brought me to Chile. Or what my fate would have been in their country. Over a Chilean cognac, we talk about fair elections and democracy, which is what they say they will have some day. How much they like Americans, but not when they are arrogant. Lucía reminds me that this home, her ancestral home, was almost confiscated under Allende's presidency. Can you imagine?

At least Pinochet brought us some stability, she means. You don't know what it was like before, she tells me. The marches, the riots, the upheaval. We were on the brink of civil war.

Realize that I am seeing a *Leave it to Beaver* life, but here it is—Latin American style. Four grown children who are highly educated, fat grandchildren and a vacation home where all can gather with little worry about mundane things like groceries, yard work and the exhaustion of house cleaning. Never a worry about money, or jobs. In this family, Lucía goes to mass every morning before work dressed in a pale linen suit, perfectly pedicured and manicured. And it's obvious to me that she and Tabo don't know any other way to live.

They criticize other families who are not as happy as they are. If only they tried harder, they hint. It is about love, they say. Like their family, *somos unidos*. Together and perfect.

I answer that I'm surprised they lasted under Pinochet, who ravaged the left, and then those who had any relationship, however distant, to people like me.

They look at each other.

Then they tell me about the day that their eldest son

was pulled off a bus in a sweep of suspected communists because he had grown a beard. How Lucía, desperate, called on her Catholic friends in high places. How they found him lined up in a dark room with other students, presided over by hooded men with rifles who were deciding who went to the left and who went to the right.

Through the intervention of her Catholic benefactor, the rifle said "go to the left." Now.

She knows that the ones on the right didn't survive. She knows this.

Lucía and Tabo give me a bottle of expensive Chilean wine to give to Josie and Jorge.

And promise to take me to visit Pablo Neruda's house tomorrow, because their second home, with a turquoise swimming pool just like this one, is only a few miles from Isla Negra.

They are neighbors.

V.
PRAY FOR US WOMEN

A Christmas Story

Leticia in handcuffs again,
arrested, smashing her husband's
windshield

Chale's been mash-potatoing her face
forever. Broke her jaw too, her face all
crooked. Leticia's boys watch the whole
show, trying not to cry while Chale tells
the cops she's the crazy one

At the other window, the German Shepherd
named Sunny barks, pushing his lion's head
through the fence, his cage, and nobody pets
him. Froze last night. Sunny walking in circles
the whole time

Outside the other window, there are boys
with skateboards, a neighbor with her cigarettes
and Coca-Cola, a homeless woman curses everyone
out under the red and green lights. Yesterday
I found a girl drinking near the trashcans,
as Leticia's husband yelled at their sons again
Dummy. Stupid. Pendejos.

Leticia calls me from jail, tells me she can't live
without her sons.

It's almost Christmas, and I'm trying to write,
but don't know this story, yet. How does it end?

The skateboarders skating
The cussing woman disappeared
Sunny got rescued thanks to you-know-who, and is
living rich
The drinking girl expelled from Jefferson

And Leticia killed herself. Left her glasses here.

There is a new dog in Sunny's yard, hungry.

The beginning of tomorrow's,

Christmas

FOR MARÍA FELIX:
WATCHING JUANA ROOSTER
ON SUNDAY AFTERNOONS

Dallas Morning News • *Oct 2000*

She strides, a black-skirted she-rooster, gun strapped on her corsetless waist. She doesn't need one, this dusty *campesina*, the peasant woman who has become a ravishing *coronela* smelling of men's blood on her boots. The ones that spark the earth once littered with dead revolutionaries like her father and fiancée, Chon.

Juana Gallo, they call her. Juana Rooster. In honor of the woman who has led an army to avenge the death of the people she loved most in the world.

Her men tremble and cheer when she speaks. Some men are afraid of her. One will die for daring her. But I think most men just fall in love despite everything. *Ay*, how I love to watch her on Sundays when people think all I do is read *The New York Times*.

Juana Rooster was a legend during the Mexican Revolution. María Felix, the actress who played her in a series of movies, was in real life a world-class diva before she died last month. In real life, *La Doña* (and nobody else could be called María in her presence) had much more interest in plastic surgery and jewels than the problems of the Mexican poor.

But in these famous movies, María depicted a peasant woman fighting for justice against the tyrants who have been Mexico's destiny, like Victoriano Huerta or Porfirio Díaz. Men who looted Mexico's treasury as ruthlessly as the Americans who stole Texas. According to my mother.

Because I was born on this side of the river, my Spanish isn't as good as my *mexicana* mother, who never lets me forget it. So I tell myself that I watch these movies to learn my language better. *Valiente.* Brave. *Enaguas.* Petticoats. *Provecho.* Benefit. *Sangre y fuego.* Blood and fire.

These movies are from Mexico's famous Golden Era, depicting a past that never was, except in my mother's imagination. A *tiempo pasado* that was mythologized, romanticized, serving as propaganda for Mexico's nationalism after the Revolution. Produced in the forties and fifties with the divine chiaroscuro of cinematographer Gabriel Figueroa (*Night of the Iguana, Under the Volcano*), they were already old when my mother took me to see them at the drive-in during the sixties.

But they were the only way she had to show me a Mexico we could rarely visit in those days. Even if the *México lindo* she remembered never existed for her. A Mexico that I keep searching for. And defending.

In *Juana Gallo,* Pioquinto the faithful (and besotted) assistant brings her a heavy gold rope of a necklace, a prize of war for the victorious beauty. She has just commanded a surprise attack, you see, that captured the *hacienda* representing all that is wrong with Mexico. Juana Rooster caresses the necklace, but not in the same way that her hands lingered over the crosses placed on the graves of her father and fiancée killed by the *federales*, General Huerta's troops. The two deaths that took her from plowing the fields as Ángela Ramos, to a colonel leading an army of men.

She falls in love, of course, but with the good bad-guy who is on Huerta's side, not *capitán* Cevallos, the chubby Zapatista-type who swaggers and sings his way into her life, conquering every woman except her. A *macho* who is a *revolucionario* like her. But Juana is aflame with the

cultured and Spanish-educated *capitán* Valverde, the elegant
enemy who prefers death rather than the cowardly option
of running when she gives him the chance. Impressed at the
bravery that matches her own, Juana lets him go free.

In the meantime, Zapata-Cevallos won't give up. Outside
her room, he croons, *eres buena o eres mala.* You give a kiss
or you shoot me. It's the same thing.

But the *federales* retake the *hacienda*, forcing Juana and
capitán Valverde—who has defected to her side—to hide in
the tunnel that winds under the building and cathedral. It
rains, there is lightning, and you-know-what happens. Then
the bad good-guy Cevallos, who can't forget her, ingeniously
storms the *hacienda* with his men. Visiting her new queen-
size bedroom, he accepts her gratitude but wants more. It
seems that the Zapatista has repented, as they always do,
since winning isn't worth much if you can't surrender your
heart. *We are at war*, he says. Then he tells her:

If I'm going to die,
my luck would be for you to kill me.
To be something in your life
if only a regret for your conscience.
That's if you have one.

Don't say that, Juana laughs at his poetics. It's true she
has killed other men, but only when they have stolen from
the people, or like those drying into beef jerky because they
killed her father and Chon. She's not like Cevallos, who
has killed for its own sake, like so many men do in battle.
Cevallos, now a three-starred colonel, knows he doesn't have
a chance, but she is so damn beautiful…though there are no
words in English or Spanish yet for this kind of woman.

I've asked other men to name an American movie star
who compares to Juana Gallo, and they are silent. You see,
Juana Rooster had the sexual wattage of Rita Hayworth with

the ferocity of Sigourney Weaver in that movie *Aliens*. Now that's my kind of Mexican woman.

I have saved a little corner for you, the large-sized Zapata-*capitán* says as he touches his heart. *Just for you. Here, inside.*

Oooh, how many corners you must have, she tosses the words like the long black braids under her traditional *rebozo. Do you say that to all the others?*

They haven't even come in.

Why would they want to go in that bottomless pit?

He is dismissed, and the Spanish *capitán* with a purer heart and track record tells her that he can't continue to stay with her—the men are calling him the "little chicken." *La gallinita* wants a transfer. He is a man, after all. Has he been a *macho* all along? Maybe she's not good enough for him. She can barely read after all, and can't walk in high heels, though she begins to practice…

The *federales* come back. After several grueling days at the final battle of Zacatecas, Cevallos is shot. A playboy to the end, he begs Juana for a goodbye kiss. As she looks up from *el beso de la despedida,* she sees that her ex-lover Valverde has witnessed this last scene from the *sangre y fuego* of war. Or the blood and fire of love. With eyes blazing, he gallops off in heartbreak, jealousy, *quien sabe.* And the next image is a field of wooden crosses.

Juana is alone. Wandering like one of those Juan Rulfo stories of desert, graves, stones and shawls. So much tragedy. All for love of country. For the love of a man.

They never learn, do they? I ask Juana Rooster. *When will they learn?*

I go to sleep.

María Antonietta Berriozábal/ Guardian Angel of San Antonio

La Voz de Esperanza • *Aug 12, 2002*

If San Antonio, Texas, is the birthplace of the Alamo, then
María Antonietta Berriozábal is the city's guardian angel.

María, as she is simply known, is a woman in her sixtieth
year who has a life-long commitment to social justice. As a
former elected official, she is that rare leader who is a spiritual force, a woman who lives by the strength of religious
convictions that are grounded in compassion and love. Happily married and childless, she nurtures the next generation
of political leaders, moving aside to give them room at the
podium. And I am writing this because she would never
write this about herself.

After decades of political activism, María became the
first Chicana councilwoman in San Antonio's history in
1981. As a woman grounded in the Church who is progressive and inclusive, she was often the lone dissenting
voice in a city surrounded then by five military bases, and a
conservative Catholic tradition encased in a violent frontier
mentality. San Antonio has a majority Latino/Chicano/
Mexican American population that is disproportionately
poor and uneducated. Its business is tourism, driven by the
cultural richness of Tex-Mex culture.

During her term on the city council, she was often at
odds with then-Mayor Henry Cisneros, who supported major development projects such as the Alamodome and tax

abatements for Sea World and Fiesta Texas. Instead, María
believed that the city should invest in human capital—in
education, health, and inner-city housing.

"Even as a little girl, I was very conscious of my environment—how the school works with the Church, how the
Church works with the neighborhood. Those relationships
fascinated me. I observed what my neighborhood looked
like—the lack of good streets, the poverty—and I would see
the rest of the city was different. I saw how hard my parents
worked. So at an early age I had a desire to work with other
people to improve my neighborhood."

During her tenure on the city council, María was a lightning rod for women's voices and concerns. She appointed
82 Latinas out of a total of 102 positions. She founded the
Hispanas Unidas Conference, and served as a presidential
appointee to the Organization of American States (OAS)
Inter-American Commission on Women. She was named
as a Fellow at the Harvard University's Institute of Politics.
Most critically, María participated in the United Nation's
Fourth International Women's Conference held in Beijing.

In 1991, after ten years as a councilwoman, she ran for
mayor. And she almost won, losing by only a few thousand
votes despite her rejection of special-interest money.

"Issues of development in San Antonio are bigger
than any local elected official… The establishment of San
Antonio is so powerful that it was, and still is, easy to get
those six votes for whatever the major business interests
want. It is very unfortunate because twenty years after our
administration of the 1980s, we are still living in a poor city,
with an ill-prepared workforce for our present technological
reality, with a brain drain of our educated youth and with
large numbers of working poor, high illiteracy and a high
dropout rate from high school."

In 1998, María ran for Congress. It was an office that many said was long overdue, and supporters expected the retiring and eminent Congressman Henry B. Gonzales to endorse her. Instead, he anointed his son, Charlie, a former judge with no political experience.

Although María has lost elections with opponents calling her "divisive," she has been victorious in her fight defending the environment, particularly the Edwards Aquifer, the city's only source of drinking water. She, along with a broad coalition of activists, twice defeated referendums against development over the recharge zone in 1991 and 1994, known as Applewhite I and Applewhite II. Joining an extraordinary coalition of women from all sectors of the city with only $12,000 against the media blast of the pro-Applewhite forces, the women-led leadership resoundingly defeated the second referendum. María's leadership was critical to the outcome.

"Sixteen White men" have all the power in San Antonio, María says, naming names as she gives her famous tour around the city to showcase the price of "economic development" with no respect for history, culture, and neighborhoods.

Recently, under María's pivotal stature, a network of environmental, neighborhood and civic organizations have forced a historic referendum in protest of another City Council decision to allow a developer to build a golf resort on the Edwards Aquifer. Because of her political and spiritual guidance, a thousand volunteers working day and night collected a record-shattering 107,032 signatures—embarrassing the mayor who only won his election with 59,000 votes.

"What is needed is support for leaders and all people on how they can integrate their life—not be people with all brains, but how they can be more compassionate and loving people. How can we talk about more love, kindness and tenderness as we change systems? I think there's incredible power in that! I look at Dorothy Day, Gandhi, César Chávez, Teresa de Ávila, who were strong people, but not political people. They were not elected to anything."

María is that rare leader who incarnates her religious heritage. Never preaching or complaining, she is the caretaker for her 90-year-old mother, as she deliberately partners her politics with the Esperanza Peace and Justice Center, a vanguard arts and cultural organization led by the media-persecuted *lesbiana* Graciela Sánchez. But most remarkably, for this day and time, María exemplifies the grace and manners that she believes a politician—and therefore, a moral leader—must have.

"One thing that is said about Latinas in leadership positions, and particularly in politics, is that we're not going to get very far because we always have the community with us. In other words, we must learn to cut the political deals. And with me, I never did it—gladly I never did it. And the reason was that when you choose that way of doing your work, you leave out the people. My work is based on listening to the people. Their clamor is for justice."

Thanks to Dr. Rudy Rosales and Mariana Ornelas for supplying some of María's comments for the writing of this article.

PRAY FOR US WOMEN

San Antonio Express-News • *June 28, 1998*

I have a problem with God.

He's always a man. And I think he hates women. Only the Southern Baptists call it obeying your husband. Catholics call it being a mother while still a virgin. Same thing. Men wrote the Bible that proves he is God. Priests who are male give us communion. Preachers, most of them men, interpret his commandments. A woman can be the mother of God. But she is never God.

"I blame the Church for our high rate of teenage pregnancies," a girlfriend argued with Father Elizondo in a debate. She was talking about a God who denies women their sexuality by idolizing an impossible virgin.

"We would welcome them in church," he says, as smooth as holy water dripping from his fingers.

Saint. Virgin. Martyr. Obey and find your reward. If we behave like Mother Teresa, or if we don't and have the good luck to die prematurely like Princess Di or Selena, then we, too, can be enshrined forever on an altar for the world to worship. No thanks. Even the Goddess of the Americas herself, our revered Virgen de Guadalupe, got passed over at the Smithsonian Conference by a priest in a prayer addressed to her son.

So much for being the mother of us all.

Yet women fill the churches on Sundays, they make the cakes for the bake sales and cook the suppers and clean the pews on Mondays. They raise their children, like my mother did, to work hard and have faith, go to college and hold important jobs and serve their husbands, family, community. Exhausted from being the perfect wife and mother, we end

up bruised from hitting the inevitable ceiling or being called
names because we dare to defend woman in all her complexity. The list is long and you probably don't know most
of them: Emma Tenayuca, María Antonietta Berriozábal,
Dr. Antonia Castañeda, Sandra Cisneros, Graciela Sánchez,
Terry Ybañez, my mother, Marina Renaud.

Be a good girl, God says. Obey. And then what?

I haven't seen one public monument to a woman in
this city, not counting the people's murals to *La Virgen* and
Selena in the *barrio*. There are great monuments to men,
Crockett, Travis, Bowie. Navarro's house is forgotten on
the other side of the river. I haven't seen any images to the
women who were their mothers, wives, teachers. And I
know they must have been in church on Sunday. Still, no
woman is good enough to have a major statue just for her. A
street with her name blazing on it that doesn't have *"Santa"*
attached to it.

Not even Jesse Treviño's depiction of the *Angel of Mercy*
that towers over Santa Rosa Hospital is female. No wonder
my mother kept changing religions: Catholic, Baptist, Assembly of God, Jehovah's Witness, looking for what doesn't
exist. A place where women are equal. A place where they
don't have to obey a man.

I know why women believe in a God who doesn't love us
the same as men. The alternative is just too frightening and
lonely. No man will love you, he threatens, at the moment
the teacher asks us to raise our hand if we know the answer
in the sixth grade, if you run faster than all the boys in the
fourth grade, if you refuse to wear makeup and shake your
nalgas at the football game. Especially if you become the
kind of woman who rebels. Who dares to question him, a
man.

"I will punish you, you will pay for this," he whispers.

"You will be alone the rest of your life. Why would a man want someone like you?"

Men are superior to women, God says. He says it in every language, in every corner of the earth. Only he doesn't really say it out loud. We say it, to each other, every time we assume *they* are better than *us*. That you are better than me. That I am better than you, because I obey.

Well, I won't. Never.

relugion patriarchy bust
L bll ppl in churcn entorce idea

COUNT ME IN

Ms. Magazine • Feb/Mar 2000

Arrested. Again. She is a 22-year-old *mujer* who is the leader of a pecan-sheller's strike in San Antonio, Texas. Over 20,000 people in the city produce half of the nation's pecan crop. The working conditions are meant to break the back and spirit. Thousands of women hear her call, and the police arrest a record number of strikers, including the leaders, most of them women. For her popularity, she is made the target of anti-union and anti-Mexican hysteria. The year is 1938. Her name is compelling, a medley of the Spanish *conquistador* and indigenous Mexican. She is Emma Tenayuca, who died last July at the age of 82.

Emma is only the latest reason many of my Latina friends have almost given up on the alternative press. Lydia Mendoza, "Songstress of the Poor," who received a National Medal of Arts in her eighth decade, is another. What about Yolanda Broyles-González, the University of California professor who was feted at the White House for winning a gender discrimination suit against the university? And the gritty Mexican runner Adriana Fernández, who won the New York City Marathon? Then there is the courage demonstrated in the *lesbiana* flesh of Graciela Sánchez, who, as the Director of the Esperanza Peace and Justice Center in San Antonio, filed a suit against the city following a homophobic campaign against the hope she believes in.

There are more where these women came from. But I don't read about them in the press that calls itself alternative. And I thought that justice was what these magazines were about.

My friends, Latinas who are writers, scholars, journal-

ists, physicians, educators, political activists, say that the
alternatives don't reflect their reality: *Utne, Mother Jones,
The Nation, Ms.* Only *The Progressive* and *Z* publish the
occasional Latina perspective. My *amigas* barely read these
magazines. No time. There is a war going on.

And it is a war that the alternatives can't win without us.
This war is between rich and poor, the many-colored and
White, women and men, straight and queer—slipping into
each other as they angle for their precarious step on the ladder. The war is about creating a society without a ladder and
the illusory weapon the status quo employs called diversity,
which is used to keep everybody wrestling for their place.

This war has exposed a deeper and more tragic battle—
the one between the so-called left and women like us, who
envision a world that listens to the lessons of its bravest.

No wonder the left is losing. No wonder *que estamos bien
jodidos*. In other words, we're totally screwed. Out-gunned
by the right's money, greed, and *Bushismo*, the left needs
the voices of women more than ever, particularly Latina
voices, which come from the battle-scarred margins. In this
war, where words are bullets meant to shatter the heart, the
left needs women who are writing from their *panochas*, the
down-there pulse of intimacy, because that's what the right
wants to destroy.

Too often, though, it's the liberal White woman and
man who have disappointed by insisting on telling us
what our story is. I want to know what *Borderlands* author
Gloria Anzaldúa thinks about public education. Ditto
for playwright lesbian-activist Cherríe Moraga and the
saga of farmworkers. I want to read Mexico's great Elena
Poniatowska in *The Nation*. Already know that I will laugh
and cry as Denise Chávez offers us Latina spirituality in
Utne. Most of all, I want to read Rigoberta Menchú's own

words as she talks about violence, forgiveness, and peace. Letting someone like me talk means that you will have to reconfigure the *mundo* we live in—bad as it is, it's all we have. But it's worth it.

If the *machismo* of the Chicano Movement taught us anything, it's that we must share or fail. My friends imagine and are fighting to create a society that embraces everyone, including White men. That's why we need a press that is truly progressive—one connected to the social movements of women all over the world who are struggling for justice. Latinas are everywhere—and nowhere. My friends in the trenches need the intellectual force that the left could give them, but doesn't. They want stories. How did other women do it? What are the ideas that inspired them? In turn, they will inspire all of us.

In the name of Emma and a thousand others who have vanished from history, I deserve to tell my story. And you deserve to hear it.

VI.
WRITE LIKE IT'S YOUR LAST DAY ON EARTH/ REVIEWS

The Secret of Bleach

Gordo soaked his feet in a bowl
of it, got rid of the fungus and
    his toenails too.
Pita's mother doesn't need the dentist
so what if her dentures look
      crooked
that's what Clorox is for, mijita
Got some trouble in your boca?
Rinse good with it.
Too many fleas on your cats outside?
Spread it around the yard with
a little water, better than Pine-Sol,
my neighbor says
Chuy swears it keeps away
the AIDS
scrub it good the morning after.

I gulped it like tequila one Christmas Eve,
mistake.
Didn't want germs in my kitchen
It won't kill you lady! 911 answers
when I say I'm gonna die come get me.

It's only bleach.

TO MY UNBORN DAUGHTER: TEJANA POETRY

La Voz de Esperanza • Mar 1999

Tejana. How proud I am to say that word. How difficult the journey to claim her.

Poetry is that *velita* that can take us to that infinite and mysterious land that is our birthright. *Entre verde y azul* goes the song by Gary Hobbs, and it is in between those borders that the poem waits to be discovered as only a Tejana can.

It was this determination to explore the emotional and spiritual territory that *Poesía Tejana* became. Conceived as a joint project between Bryce Milligan, in his capacity as an independent publisher of Wings Press, and the financial and creative *bendición* of Sandra Cisneros, Tejana extraordinaire who received a MacArthur "genius grant" in 1995 for her poetry and fiction, *Poesía Tejana* has pushed the next generation of Tejana poets into the forefront of the literary landscape.

And if you can judge a book by its cover, the Tejanas, wings beating, are ready to *dale shine* and fly. Original to the bone, the Poesía Tejana Prize will be given to four Tejana poets (Latinas living in Texas under the age of 30) each year. The prize consists of a series of published chapbooks, one for each winner, immaculately bound, sculpted, printed, then painted with artist Terry Ybañez's *lotería*-styled depiction of an open hand shaded by the thicker finger-leaves of the *maguey* cactus, a beauty to see and hold. For this first year of 1999, four poets, Victoria García-Zapata, Celeste Guzmán, Mary Grace Rodríguez, and Nicole Pollentier, have been honored with the limited-edition publication of their respective work, along with a $100 cash award.

A disclaimer: I know three of these women. Another disclaimer: I never had a daughter. It is a pleasure to have watched these women explore their lives, fired by their heritage, emblazoned by their gifts. All four women have written personal poems, not political ones. This is not the fisted hand striking out at injustice, a Tejana righteous with rage. No, these poems are the hand sketches of family, *picante* and loving, mothers and fathers, brothers and uncles, lovers and grandmothers, who made them Tejanas. Ms. Pollentier is the notable exception, using the cycle of salmon as her metaphor and book cover's emblem.

It is the banner of family or fish that illuminates the poems, as it shields the poets from their difficult path. Because it is the most terrifying thing of all to choose a poet's life. South of the border and across the world, poets fill stadiums and are treated as royalty. Pablo Neruda read to the miners, who stood for hours to hear him. His poems are literally music, now universally known whenever a guitarist joins the group in Latin America. Poets are also killed and tortured, many sit in jails as prisoners because they dared to write a poem that asked, why? In Texas, our poets are as spare as the land. And the women? They are the *mesquite*, like Ángela De Hoyos, rooted deep and clinging to the earth because they refuse to give up. They have not counted, because they belong here.

Another disclaimer: I can't write poetry. These women obviously can, and the responsibility they carry is great. The bravest is Victoria García-Zapata, (*Peace in the Corazón*), who confronts the brutality of a man against a woman and finds a hard-earned independence. The funkiest is Celeste Guzmán, (*Cande, te estoy llamando),* who remembers the women in her family who sighed and dreamed, as she struggles to prove to her father that she can catch a baseball, too. The most tantalizing is Mary Grace Rodríguez's *Long Story Short,* who mourns her lost loves as sadly as her lost history. And Nicole Pollentier's *Smolt* is the dreamcatcher, as she finds allusions between the men in her life and the coming and going of fish, cats, Evel Knievel.

The poetry that each woman offers us, inspired and elegant, *barrioized* and tender, tells us more about her, about us, by what she does not tell. But the hints are there. I have faith that each one of these *cabronas* has the *huevos* to claim what's hers. Texas is a big place, and we need poems as fierce, as passionate, as courageous as the land we come from.

A final disclaimer: Because I didn't have a daughter, I realize how each one of these women is my *hija,* too, burdened with a future I will never know. In Celeste Guzmán's final poem "To My Unborn Daughter," she imagines the child she will have someday:

When you take root inside me
I will fill the world differently
belly and breasts
growing larger and larger

When you push yourself out into
the San Antonio air
you will scream loud, I think in
exaltation
that our eyes will finally meet
and for that one moment
we will know each other.

Daughters of ink and paper, blood and land, I am waiting.

José Antonio Burciaga/ Spilling the Beans

San Antonio Express-News • *1996*

This is a story about José Antonio Burciaga, a great writer, who died of cancer on October 7, 1996. Because he wrote about me. And you. And from his story comes my own.

I used to be a *gringa*. In a place where the twilight is a good day, where a bad day is one long hot eclipse. That's when I was someone else. Because I had to survive. I grew up in *el norte*, in Olton, under the neck of the Texas Panhandle, at a time when the Whites were the farmers and men like my father were the farmworkers. There was nothing in between.

The eight years I spent in that place was like falling under a broken merry-go-round. Like when my hands slipped from the handlebars, and the others kicked me as I spun in the dirt. Because there was so much hate between the Whites and the rest of us. Sometimes it was so loud that I began to believe I really was a greasy-good-for-nothing-bean-eating dirty Mexican. Stupid and lazy spic, eating her *tortillas* in the corner. If everyone hated me, there had to be a good reason. It was only in school that this *chata*-faced Latina could hate them back. To prove that I was somebody. To be better than them.

And I escaped. To *el sur*, back to South Texas on my father's back when he was cheated out of the harvest due to him. At fourteen, I transferred to Del Río San Felipe High School, and saw what Latinos could achieve. Because the whole world is Latino there. I began to understand what my Mexican mother told me about her side of things, my

history, my *español*. It was there that I fell in love with my
people. I was home. I became a *Tejana con gas.*

But still I did not know. Because I did not know my
stories. *Claro*, I knew about Dreiser's great "American Tragedy" story of class. I learned about the odyssey of the soul
from Homer, crime and guilt from Dostoevsky and passion
a la Tennessee Williams. From King Lear to Christopher
Columbus. I knew those stories. But it was never enough. I
ached for something else. I would buy all the so-called great
books, joined the book clubs, but it was like drinking my
own blood. The Latin American masters like Borges and
Neruda helped, but their intimacy in Spanish only served to
show me how ignorant I was. Because none of these stories
told me what I did not know how to ask.

They did not tell me about my story.

*We ate the freshly made frijoles de la olla, we ate them in
different recipes: frijoles borrachos, frijoles charros, frijoles
sencillos…we ate enfrijoladas, like enchiladas but soaked in
beans instead of chile, we had tacos de frijoles, bean burritos,
tostadas de burritos, refried in sandwiches and even mat-
zohs or bagels smothered with refried beans. We scrambled
them with eggs, we ate them with diced jalapeños, nopalitos,
chorizo, melted cheese…you name it. We ate frijoles when its
soup thickened. We ate them when the refried beans had just
about dried up.*
—From *Spilling the Beans* by José Antonio Burciaga

Just write it down. So simple, so hard to do. But that is
exactly what he did. José Antonio Burciaga, writer, winner
of a 1995 Hispanic Heritage Award in Literature, was *muy*
witty and a better humorist than even Will Rogers. Burciaga
had the political *tripas* of Molly Ivins or Jim Hightower,

but with brown Chicano soul. His artistic legacy, brave and completely authentic, serves as a cultural beacon to the Latino world.

But be careful when calling someone a pendejo. Among friends it can be taken lightly, but for others it is better to be angry enough to back it up. Ironically, the Yiddish word for pendejo is a putz which means the same thing.
—From "Pendejismo," in *Drink Cultura*

***

At Casa Zapata, the students heard their stories for the first time. Burciaga recognized that his students were intellectually gifted, but starving for their culture. So he told them a story that would transform them, by painting a mural at Casa Zapata that depicted a famous supper as he knew it. And swore to cover Stanford with more.

***

Burciaga proved to have a brush as mighty as his pen. In his acclaimed work, *Last Supper of Chicano Heroes*, Burciaga interpreted the religious figures of the "Lord's Last Supper" as a cosmic table of Latino heroes. And he revealed who is important to Latinos and Chicanos in the America that we know. Sitting at the table are fourteen disciples for justice: César Chávez, Martin Luther King, Dolores Huerta, Benito Juárez, Ricardo Flores Magón, Ernesto Galarza, Emiliano Zapata and Joaquín Murrieta; revolutionary artists like the Mexican nun Sor Juana Inés de la Cruz, Frida Kahlo and Luís Valdez; vanguard educators like former UCLA Chancellor Tomás Rivera. Che Guevara holds court in

the middle. Naturally, *la* Virgen de Guadalupe is blessing
them. President Kennedy and his brother Robert are in the
audience, accompanied by Tejano General Ignacio Zara-
goza. Chilean Gabriela Mistral and the ordinary workers
who scrubbed floors so that we could go to college. Just like
my own father and mother. They are heroes because they
worked hard every day so that we would not suffer. And *La
Muerte* is there too as the Angel of Mercy, because she is the
heroine of death who will avenge our lives.

*A corazonaso can be: a dolor de corazón—heartache; corazón
partido—heartbreak; corazón doloroso—heart-rending.*
—"Lo del corazón," from Undocumented Love/Amor Indoc-
umentado

The Chicano griot never stopped writing. He said that
the denial of his Spanish forced him to write because he
had to speak. And Burciaga wrote with all the words at his
disposal: the ancient Aztec Nahuatl, Spanish, Tex-Mex,
the *pachuco's Caló* and always the carnivorous English.
He wrote about NAFTA, immigration, Quetzalcoatl, and
tortillas as the first Frisbees with *guato* and wisdom. *Órale*,
Mark Twain.

Burciaga was not afraid to tell. He went to war for us
with his stories full of *corazón* and other *desmadres*. Because
he showed us how a *tortilla* can save us. Or a *jalapeño*. He
was not afraid of our hearts breaking with the Spanish we
had lost, with the poignancy of our American journey. And
he put it all down in the stories that we had almost forgotten. *Con safos.*

The truth is that I tire,
I tire of yelling,

I tire of writing,
I tire of painting,
but know nothing except
to yell, write, and paint
—"The Truth," from *Undocumented Love/Amor Indocumen-*
tado

EDUARDO GALEANO/
THE TRUTH BE TOLD:
EDUARDO GALEANO DISPELS
MYTHS OF HISTORY

San Antonio Express-News • Apr 1999

Most people would rather not remember the past because the present is difficult enough. *No quiero saber, cállate.* Our history is today, and tomorrow is already forgetting. Another's suffering is not my *problema*. It has nothing to do with me.

But there are those whose fate it is to give us back our memory. One is the writer Eduardo Galeano of Montevideo in Uruguay, a country so small and far away that most of us don't know exactly where it is or what has happened there. But writing with a pen made of fire, he makes us see that there is here, that yesterday has begun again. That each of our stories is different, yet the very same. So that we can dream with our eyes open.

Throughout Latin America, Galeano is revered and feared because he is obsessed with writing the story of the Americas, spilling its secrets, sacred, tragic, heroic, in a voice exquisite as its people. A wretched history student in school, he wants to rescue the memory of America from the museums and statues, lectures and medals of those who tell us what history should be, not what it is.

His astonishing dozen-plus books have been published in more than 20 languages, a treasury of essays, journalism, and history that reflects what he says is a "reality of Latin America...more fantastic than the lies we've been told," because "nothing is more horrible or poetic than the truth."

For this, some say he will win the Nobel Prize for literature. For he has written what is impossible, saved history from itself. That possibility is his masterpiece, *Memory of Fire*, a trilogy that tells the story of America from its creation myths to the myth of conquest, the centuries of resistance and the monsters that shadow our modernity.

Written during a long exile abroad, it is a wholly original composition of historical facts rendered into almost a thousand pages of flesh and blood. Galeano has taken the scraps of our stories and rewoven them into an epic of multiple narratives and calendars. Under Galeano, our history has been realized as a story that deserves to be told with the force of magic and the grace of prophecy.

"It is just that our story is too beguiling to be drowned by dates," he says. In *Memory of Fire* we can hear the clacking of God's *maracas* as he dreams the first man and woman; smell the stained velvet cape that Christopher Columbus brandishes as he takes his first walk on the beach at Guanahani; touch the mangled neck of the beheaded Incan leader Tupac Amaru in Cuzco, Perú, in 1572; taste the cotton buds, bitter as slavery, that bring the Anglo settlers across the prairie to Texas. We marvel at the perfect explosion of the plane carrying the Argentine Carlos Gardel and his tragic *tangos* to death in 1935.

Galeano has transparent eyes, says another writer, and there is nothing you can hide from him. Born into a family anchored in Uruguay for several generations, Eduardo Hughes Galeano is the descendant of immigrants who defends the native heritage of America. He has grandparents from Great Britain, Italy, Spain and Germany and the face of the Swedish consul in Honduras, he says. At 14, he entered the world of journalism because of a political cartoon he drew for the *Socialist Weekly* of Montevideo. Signing his

name "Gius," from the Spanish pronunciation of the Hughes
that came from his Welsh great-grandfather, he alternated
between drafting and journalism.

At 18, he wanted to write from the heart, with everything,
he says, and so he died and was born again. At 20 he wrote a
bad novel signing it Galeano, his mother's last name, which
came to him from a great-grandfather from Genoa.

He was surrounded by an enlightened family, says my
friend Manuela, who remembers his sister's classroom where
she was a student in the years before she was jailed under the
military dictatorship. It was her generation that Galeano inspired to protest when he was chief of the weekly *Marcha* and
daily *Epoca*. In 1973, the military closed congress, banned the
Communist Party and other left-wing groups and censured
the press. Escaping to Buenos Aires, Galeano founded and
led the magazine *Crisis*. It was his fate to live as his colleagues
were tortured and disappeared in Argentina's "Dirty War."
Written for death by the military, he escaped again, this time
to an exile of eight years in Spain, returning to Montevideo in
1985 *donde no lo sacan ni madre*. Just try and get him to leave
his home, says his agent and friend, Susan Bergholz.

It is the fate of Galeano to write the story of the Americas
for those who could not, to breathe life into them so that
we will know what they wanted to tell us before they died.
Galeano discovers the story that has been erased from
history, the chains dancing in spite of the shackled feet and
wrists as the Africans walk wrapped in dignity from the
slave ships. The desperate story, struggling to survive like the
Indian woman brutally raped by the *conquistador* Miguel de
Cuneo, who recorded it with vicious pleasure.

With Galeano beside us, we hear the courageous story
of the Reverend Martin Luther King Jr. when he says from a
balcony in Memphis that the United States is suffering from

an infection of the soul, and that the name of that infection is Vietnam. Then a bullet rips his face, but not his legacy.

To read Galeano is to find one's place in America. And that place is braided into each other's lives, looped with conquest, tied together like Rigoberta Menchú's *trenzas*. Each story is a piece of our inheritance.

There is Manuela Sáenz, the woman left behind to scandal when Simón Bolívar flees Colombia; the gentlemen who dress in the newest French styles in Chile; the Irishmen of Mexico City who come as invaders and die for the invaded; the message to the White man from Chief Seattle that "you people will suffocate in your own waste"; the Mexican Indian President Juárez, who is convinced that if Mexico copies enough, she too will be a great nation; the Nicaraguan peon, Augusto César Sandino, short and skinny as maize, who listens to what the land tells him he must do; the Chicanos working the fields in San José, California, who nobody wants except when there is war.

Galeano doesn't write for you or me, but for those who cannot read. The inequality of Latin America, he believes, means that the fate of Latin American writers is linked to the need for profound social transformation.

In Latin America, censorship exists, he says, because the majority of the people cannot afford to buy books. In the United States, the censorship is more subtle, as the mind is drugged, the soul is withered by the consumption of goods and the illusions of television. Here we have flashy cars but our history has been consigned to the junkyard of our imagination. But there is gold in that trash. "Memory can save us," says Galeano. So he writes about who we are, capturing the intimate moments that make the past the present and the future a repetition of the beginning or a window on hope. So that we can know what we deserve to become.

Cultural bridges and mixes fill Chicana's writing

This Bridge We Call Home: Radical Visions for Transformation
Edited by Gloria E. Anzaldúa and AnaLouise Keating
Routledge, $24.95 paper

BY BÁRBARA RENAUD GONZÁLEZ
SPECIAL TO THE EXPRESS-NEWS

She was destined to write. The signs were there, beginning with her bleeding at three months of age. A migrant child of Texas in the '50s and '60s, Gloria Anzaldúa grew up on a ranchito outside Edinburg. The experience of knowing differences — this living on the border, as a living bridge between childhood and adulthood, north and south, the only honor student in a white classroom where *mexicanos* struggled with school — would transform her into one of the country's leading radical thinkers.

An independent scholar and writer, Anzaldúa is a *nepantlera*, a woman who lives in the middle of many worlds. A leading figure in feminist, Chicano and queer studies around the country, her books are very widely cited, and hailed for advancing an integrated discussion on race, class, sexuality and gender.

Anzaldúa, who will give a read-

ing tonight at the Esperanza Peace and Justice Center, freely mines the personal into astonishing theoretical constructs that are grounded in her woman's spirituality, lesbian *grario/go* and what she calls her indigenous/Chicana *historieta*. She speaks simply and urgently about if it is to be whole, if we demand if it is to be whole. With the anthology "This Bridge Called My Back" (cowritten with Cherríe Moraga, Third Woman Press 2002), Anzaldúa challenged the narrow perspectives of traditional white feminism, creating instead a bridge between and for women of color. She continued her exploration of the bridge into the internal psychic borders we have yet to cross in "Borderlands/La frontera: The New Mestiza" — selected as one of the 100 best books of the 20th century by the *Utne Reader*.

In her new anthology, "This Bridge We Call Home," Anzaldúa takes us yet another step toward a soulful consciousness she defines as *conocimiento* by constructing a bridge of possibility to the rest of the world. She and co-editor and fellow *nepantlera* Ana-

Louise Keating (an associate professor of women's studies at Texas Woman's University) have collected the stories of more than 80 contributors in a 500-page manifesto that realizes the transformative potential of *mestizaje* (mixed people) illuminated by travelers who have crossed many different bridges.

Anzaldúa and Keating take it even further than the definition of mixed-blood that is in vogue today, considering the mixed-culture and mixed-gender realities that have people in a *nepantla* state — the border, the emotional land between us and them.

Organized into seven stages of bridge-building, "This Bridge Called Home" expands beyond women of color to include whites, transsexual (Max Wolf Valerio, "Now that you're a White Man: Changing Sex in a Postmodern World"); the fat, the Jewish, the straight, Native American, South Asian/Indian, an Arab American

feminist.

From her home in Norway, San Antonio native Susan Guerra's essay ("In the End, We are All Chicanas") speaks of the unfinished promises of reconciliation.

"My friend Malika knows what the experts don't. Her kids learned Arabic and Norwegian from birth. With all the attachments to the languages too! Couscous filling their nostrils, steam in their dark brown curls as they hear mama Malika talk that dynamic language sounding like cinnamon bark and whole clove stems being crumbled into a casserole — and the Norwegian pans setting knives and forks on the dinner table, joking and laughing in that language of tonal hills, snowy slopes, deep icy fjords, and red apple orchard valleys. His languages right alongside the Arabic ... The bobble tail of words floats off. The essays, while drawing to

look at from its placid cover and heft, are accessible if one reads, I suspect, as Anzaldúa writes — in bits and pieces, freely, without the teacher in the room.

It's not enough to denounce the world's tribal culture, concludes Anzaldúa. You must provide new narratives that embody alternative potentials. That's why she reclaims the phrase "new tribalism" as an identity of *mestizaje* that propagates other world views, spiritual traditions, and cultures to your tree of life. In this way we can rewrite the story of the "fall" and the story of Western progress — two opposing versions of the evolution of human consciousness.

Collectively, the new *mestizaje*

can birth the emergence of a new world's wisdom. I learned from her that my multidimensional and multilayered life can be a bridge to the common person within the puzzle of our humanity. So that I can break down the walls like the one in Berlin. So that I can find home.

Gloria E. Anzaldúa and Ana-Louise Keating, along with contributors Liliana Wilson Grez and Susan Guerra, will read from and discuss "This Bridge We Call Home." 7:9 tonight at the Esperanza Peace and Justice Center. Anzaldúa also will appear at 5 solo "Tertulia" event at 7 p.m. Friday. Suggested admission is $3-$5 for each event.

GLORIA ANZALDÚA/ THIS BRIDGE WE CALL HOME

*San Antonio Express-News • *Nov 2002*

This Bridge We Call Home
Edited by Gloria E. Anzaldúa & Ana Louise Keating
Routledge (Sep 2002)

She was destined to write. The signs were there, beginning
with her bleeding at three months of age. A migrant child
of Texas in the '40s and '50s, Gloria Anzaldúa grew up on
a *ranchito* outside Edinburg. The experience of knowing
differences—this living on the border, as a living bridge
between childhood and adulthood, north and south; the
only honor student in a White classroom where *mexicanos*
struggled with school—would transform her into one of the
country's leading radical thinkers.

An independent scholar and writer, Anzaldúa is a
nepantlera, a woman who lives in the middle of many
worlds. A leading figure in feminist, Chicana and queer
studies around the country, her books are widely cited,
studied and admired for advancing an integrated discussion
on race, class, sexuality and gender.

Anzaldúa, who will give a reading tonight at the
Esperanza Peace and Justice Center, freely mixes the
personal into astonishing theoretical constructs that are
grounded in her woman's spirituality lesbian geography and
what she calls her indigenous/Chicana *historería*. She speaks
simply and urgently about making the world more feminine
if it is to be whole.

With the anthology *This Bridge Called My Back* (co-

edited with Cherríe Moraga, Third Woman Press 2002),
Anzaldúa challenged the narrow perspectives of traditional
White feminism, creating instead a bridge between and
for women of color. She continued her exploration of the
bridge into the internal psychic borders we have yet to cross
in *Borderlands/La Frontera: The New Mestiza*—selected as
one of the 100 best books of the 20th century by *The Utne
Reader*.

In her new anthology *This Bridge We Call Home*,
Anzaldúa takes us on yet another step toward a soulful
consciousness by constructing a bridge of possibility to the
rest of the world. She and co-editor and fellow *nepantlera*
Ana Louise Keating (an associate professor of Women's
Studies at Texas Women's University) have collected
the stories of more than 80 contributors in a 500-page
manifesto that realizes the transformative potential of
mestizaje (mixed people) illuminated by travelers who have
crossed many different bridges.

Anzaldúa and Keating take it even further than the
definition of mixed-blood that is in vogue today, considering the mixed-culture and mixed-gender realities that leave
people in a *nepantla* state—the border, the middle land
between us and them.

Organized into seven stages of bridge-building, *This
Bridge We Call Home* expands beyond women of color to
include White, transsexual (Max Wolf Valero, *Now That
You're a White Man: Changing Sex in a Postmodern World*);
the fat, the Jewish, the straight, Native American, South
Asian/Indian, an Arab-American feminist.

From her home in Norway, San Antonio native Susan
Guerra's essay ("In the End, We are all Chicanas") speaks of
the unfinished promises of reconciliation.

My friend Malika knows what the experts don't. Her

*kids learned Arabic and Norwegian from birth. With all
the attachments to the languages too! Couscous filling their
nostrils, steam in their dark brown curls as they hear mama
Malika talk that dynamic language sounding like cinnamon
bark and whole clove stems being crumbled into a casserole...
and the Norwegian papa setting knives and forks on the
dinner table, joking and laughing in that language of tonal
hills, snowy slopes, deep icy fjords, and red apple orchard
valleys, the langu-edge, right alongside the Arabic... The
bubble ball of words floats off the tongue and rolls and rolls
and rolls.*

The essays, while daunting to look at from the placid
cover and heft, are accessible if one reads, I suspect, as
Anzaldúa writes—in bits and pieces, freely, without the
teacher in the room.

It's not enough to denounce the world's tribal cultures,
concludes Anzaldúa. You must provide new narratives that
embody alternative potentials. That's why she reclaims the
phrase "new tribalism" as an identity of *mestizaje* that propagates other world views, spiritual traditions, and cultures
to your tree of life. In this way we can rewrite the story of
"the fall" and the story of Western progress—two opposing
versions of the evolution of human consciousness.

Collectively, the new *mestizaje* can birth the emergence
of a new world's wisdom. I learned from her that my multidimensional and multilayered life can be a bridge to the
common prisons within the puzzle of our humanity. So that
I can break down the walls like the one in Berlin. So that I
can find home.

DANIELA ROSSELL/
RICAS Y FAMOSAS

Editorial Oceano/Turner • *2002*

Ricas y Famosas: México 1994–2001
By Daniela Rossell
Turner (Aug 2002)

Believe me, I am not qualified to write a review about a photographic gallery of the scandalously rich and self-imagined famous women of Mexico. I come from a family where high school graduation portraits followed by baby-faced soldiers shine from dime-store frames, proudly surrounded by souvenir ashtrays from Oklahoma, insurance calendars, and a giant pink-porcelain *concha* from Tampico that was the prized family heirloom. In my house, Avon collectibles were considered fine art.

¿Qué sé yo? Who am I to say that this photographic survey is a brilliant and penetrating journey into desire, consumption, beauty and post-modern delirium? Especially when the upper-class and *gringo*-educated Mexican media sneers at the depravity of the *rasquache* descendants of the Mexican revolutionary elite. This is Mexico, remember, and the many fetishized blonde *mexicanas* photographed amidst acres of stuffed toys, stuffed hunting trophies from Africa, blackamoor statuary, Catholic crosses and Guadalupes, colonial empire art replete with sacked-cathedral pews and archbishop chairs, Zapata's oil-painted visage and commissioned portraits of these women preening in their baroque palaces of marble floors, silk pillows and Target trash cans is no more or less a reflection of our conflicted and collective history. They are *no-*

sotros, I'm afraid. They just have more money than my family.

And while I'm at it, let me say from my *barrioesque* perspective that these women are about as outrageous as Moctezuma's kingdom of gold, blood, and quetzal feathers. Or Hernán Cortez's land-grabbing scheme that afforded him the next one. Sound familiar in San Anto?

Fortunately, Daniela Rossell is truly outrageous. She is the 29-year-old established photographer and granddaughter of two former Mexican governors whose close and extended family is depicted in this kinky family album of the Rovirosa-Rossell clan of Mexico. The lush photographs constitute an eight-year project that began with her inner-circle clan in Mexico City and expanded from there to include relatives and friends throughout Mexico, New York City, and San Antonio. The what-have-I-done-to-deserve-this-controversy Rossell is the daughter of Haydee Rovirosa and Guillermo Rossell, and it is her own grandparents posing in their gilded cupola as they celebrate their fiftieth wedding anniversary.

The photographs, says artist Franco Mondini, a San Antonio native who lives in New York and who was selected for the prestigious Whitney Biennial last year, are unquestionably harmonic, nuanced, symbolically rich and to his eyes, subversive. As an artist whose work plies the warring aesthetics of *mestizo* culture, Mondini refuses to accept the waspy North American model (i.e., anti-purple house) as the superior hallmark for good taste over the vibrant coats of poverty. "Your house has to look like London?" What constitutes elegant restraint? he wonders. "In the U.S., we're using half of the world's resources...at least do it right."

The question, says cultural anthropologist Marta Turok, a "dryback" whose American parents chose to live in Mexico, is "she grew up in this...is she reflecting her reality, does she realize the profundity of the document that she produced?"

In Mexico, Turok confesses, "we know how they came about their money." She assumes I am aware that the revolutionary government Partido Revolucionario Institucional (PRI) looted the treasury and disenfranchised the hopes of the million people who died in it—"we just didn't know how they spent it."

But Rossell's most shattering observations are about women as creatures (a few men, including Emiliano Salinas, the son of the exiled Mexican president donning a priestly pose, are exceptions). The photographs capture women as extreme-sport fantasies of men. I am thankful that Rossell's mind-blowing wealth allows me to see exactly what men get for their (my ancestors') money—Stepford-wife dolls, queens and princesses from the royal ambitions of the *conquistadores*, golden bad girls, a *vaquera* in red hot-pants, safari-set dominatrixes, blondes, blondes, did I say blondes? Because these photographs represent more than the past era of the ruling PRI's materialistic vampirism—they are a woman's sad imitation of her own perverse consumption: reflected in the movies, in the *telenovelas,* in the fashion magazines of how she must be.

Such is the legacy of conquest. Rossell protests too much. She knew damn well what she was doing.

You want a peek? There is a modern-day harem underneath an Arabic mural of another harem; a golden woman perched on a golden Buddha beside a pool of champagne and money; gay and lesbian soft erotica; a Chinese vidette and one black s*antería*-looking priestess. One *morena*—reminiscent of a brown-skinned Lolita reclining in fishnet stockings and poker-card skirt. And not one of these women is dressed like Jackie Kennedy Onassis, ok? But if I remember my history correctly, the vaunted fortunes of the Carnegies and Rockefellers did not exactly come from clean hands either. The Ivy

League manicure comes much later.

From the first to the last page, this photographic *testimonio* proves that contemporary art can have a ferocious impact if you find the velvet interior of politics. It could not have been an easy task for Rossell to pose her trusting subjects and their prized objects in what became the subtle overlapping and intersecting thematic arrangements of this book: the conquest of land, the appropriation of God, women, animals, natives, and the dark feminization of men. No one and nothing is spared. Even the Revolution has been conquered. The unhinged lust is there for all of us to see what each and everyone of us is capable of. For in the faces of these startling and naked hungers, I can see traces of myself.

The final image is the masterstroke. Seated between two giant ivory tusks on gleaming Italian stairs, thirty-three servants encircle their *patrón*, each one holding a possession of his while the boss holds a silvery sheet of dollar bills. Silicone chips? Whatever it is, he holds it close to his body as the uniformed retinue around him displays all that he owns. As he owns them. How many of those somber human possessions, if history repeats itself, would do the same thing if they were the master, given a chance? How many would become Zapata?

Ten percent of Mexico's people control forty percent of the nation's wealth. Over half of the population lives in a kind of poverty that most of us could not stomach if we could see it, but we won't. And such is the polarity that the United States keeps pushing toward with the steady dismantlement of our middle class. In century after century, from Miguel Hidalgo to Pancho Villa to NAFTA, the misery of Mexico grows and flows into the Río Grande. A lesson for us—if we are willing to learn from a conquered people: It is not how you spend your money, but how you share it that matters.

Therein lies wealth.

DENISE CHÁVEZ/
LOVING PEDRO INFANTE:
THE MORNING AFTER

San Antonio Express-News • *Feb 27, 2001*

Loving Pedro Infante
By Denise Chávez
Washington Square Press (Mar 2001)

Eliberto, my Pedro Infante, once told me that those of us who live on the border, between two worlds, love our food greasy because it makes our lives delicious when living here is so tragic.

It is no wonder, then, that in Denise Chávez's latest and best *novela*, the searching for love scorches and burns like a #5 Combination Plate at midnight. But *ay,* how good it tastes going down. Pedro Infante was a movie star and singer as close to a Mexican god as you can get after that feathered-serpent Quetzalcoatl left us promising to return. That god took to the east by sea, but Pedro Infante flew his own plane, crashed, and died on April 15, 1957, at age forty.

Though, like Elvis, he has been sighted all over Mexico and even on the border at twilight.

Once idol and now myth, Pedro Infante is the kind of man that Tere Ávila and Irma *"La Wirms"* Granados, *las* girlfriends—and protagonists—of this book, are searching for. But he has proven elusive to find in their little dusty town of Cabritoville, USA. Or at La Tempestad, the *rasquache* bar they visit on weekends, where Tere gets good and *borracha,* where they reminisce about past loves, pick up men, only to wake up lonelier than ever. Yes, they are *pu-*

tas, a big black P plastered on their foreheads, Tere admits. And what does that make the men? Then Tere meets Lucio, a married man with a daughter he loves as much as she wishes her late father had loved her. With his *nalga*-hugging straight-leg jeans and pigskin Luccheses, she has found her Pedro Infante.

I once heard a girlfriend tell me that she was so passionate about a certain man that her panties—just melted off. That's how *caliente* the relationship is between Tere and Lucio. After all, she has seen all of Pedro Infante's sixty-two films, and as vice-president in good standing of the Pedro Infante Fan Club #256, visits his grave site yearly. Tere's father died when she was very young, you see. And now divorced, and in her thirties, she is as hungry for love as she is for those red *enchiladas* from Sofía's Mighty Taco.

In this *teatro* of a book, Denise Chávez uses her considerable skills as an actress and playwright to offer us a cinematic story that is juicy with sweat and intrigue. Buttery as popcorn and semen. Nothing, I mean nothing, is as sacred to Chávez as the body. There are places in this book that are so indulgent—and so fattening—that you won't be able to put it down as the affair tantalizes your soul and your *panza*.

As Tere is the body, her best friend, Irma *"La Wirms,"* is the intellect. Chávez portrays these women as the beautiful, enduring, and intelligent women we know our real-life girlfriends to be. Can't we talk about something besides men, Irma demands of Tere in the midst of her affair with Lucio, like art or culture perhaps?

But just like in real life, our girlfriends are more obsessed with finding the perfect man who is just like the father who wasn't. If *Loving Pedro Infante* has any faults, it is this lack of examination into Tere's devouring of a man to complete her as a woman. It is the one essential ingredient missing, like not enough *jalapeños* in the *caldo,* the internal scorching that is required to transform Tere into a woman who can embrace herself so that she won't have to be searching for a man like her father or Pedro Infante to embrace her instead.

But who needs to talk about Daddy when you have a girlfriend who will pick you up when Pedro betrays you as they always do? Chávez's *brava* story of love affirms women, Latinas, and the whole of our lives—our jobs, our faith, our tight dresses when we go to the *baile.* For this alone, she has earned her place at the most elegant table of American letters.

So leave him, *comadre.* Forget him. Believe in yourself. And your Pedro Infante might appear when you least expect it. Because you aren't searching for anyone, but yourself.

Now, pass the *salsa.*

ALMA GUILLERMOPRIETO/
LOOKING FOR HISTORY:
DISPATCHES FROM
LATIN AMERICA

San Antonio Express-News • May 14, 2001

Looking for History: Dispatches from Latin America
Alma Guillermoprieto
Vintage (later edition, Mar 2002)

> *Si el norte era el sur…*
> —Ricardo Arjona, Guatemalan singer

If the north was south and the south was north, we might begin to understand each other. That's the *esperanza* that Alma Guillermoprieto shares in her third book on Latin America, and she is superbly qualified to offer it. Based in Mexico City, she writes for *The New Yorker* magazine, and is the winner of journalism's highest prizes, and most recently, the recipient of a MacArthur "genius" grant in 1995.

In this book of seventeen essays, Guillermoprieto's ferocious intellect and woman's intuition continues to illuminate the people and politics of the south, looking for history in places that many others haven't gone, or miss because they just don't know what to look for. But she does. She is from there.

Looking for a deeper understanding of history through the interplay of reportage and her intimate gaze, she sifts through some of Latin America's most provocative legends and countries. At once sweeping and graceful, she exam-

ines Argentina's Eva Perón, Ernesto "Che" Guevara, Fidel
Castro, and Perú's failed presidential candidate and world-
class writer, Mario Vargas-Llosa. All were shaped by their
experiences with class prejudice which is Latin America's
particular brand of racism, reveals Guillermoprieto, telling
us without telling us. They are their history, she makes us
see.

In lengthier and more voluptuous essays, she turns her
mexicana's eyes toward the prostitution of Cuba's *Fidelismo*,
suffering from its crumbling ideals and mansions, now
selling the flesh of her beautiful *mulatas*. Compellingly,
she examines the intricacies and interstices of Colombia's
violent and magical past, present and future. Violence is the
real drug of Colombia, she discovers. Finally, she spotlights
her own Mexico—and its labyrinthine and revolutionary
journey to *Foxanadú*.

It is one thing to understand your neighbor, but it is
another to understand yourself. In her hundred-plus pages
on Mexico, Guillermoprieto's critical eye examines her
home through the backdrop of three murders: the killing of
PRI chief José Francisco Ruiz Massieu, the assassination of
PRI presidential candidate Luís Donaldo Colosio, and the
machine-gun slaying of the Archbishop Cardinal Juan Jesús
Posadas at the Guadalajara airport in the mid-nineties.
None of these murders have been resolved to any satis-
faction, and Guillermoprieto considers how each one is a
symptom of Mexico's failed revolution—the steadfast and
corrupting Partido Revolucionario Institucional (PRI).

But, like the mother who can't admire her son's accomplishments for picking at his flaws, Guillermoprieto's
gaze falters in her scrutiny of the ones who have not been
given enough credit for changing Mexico's history—the
Zapatistas. In her chapters on this subject, "Zapata's Heirs,"

and "The Unmasking," she challenges their idealism, their myth-making Subcomandante Marcos, as she traces their abject poverty, their marginalization from Mexican society, their unceasing claim to land and liberty.

In a middle-of-the-night interview with Marcos himself, she is disappointed when she realizes that he is a utopian..."dealing with closed universities, good and evil, and dreaming of egalitarian, redeeming poverty just as the visionary church does, or the *campesino* communities so eager to pursue a vision of hope." Here the super-journalist who has everything, reveals her own history. She is afraid of what freedom might mean.

"Is it a crime to want what they want?" say the *campesinos* in response to her questions that they be more practical. "We are ignorant," says a woman to her in broken Spanish. "But...do the bourgeois, the rich people's children, sleep on the floor, the way ours do? Do helicopters come and terrify them?"

Can we see history when it is being made in front of our very eyes? Yes. And no, if we are the ones inside it.

Under Guillermoprieto's exquisite and all-too-human gaze, the South is not so different from the North after all.

THE TARGETING OF CHICANO!

The Progressive Magazine • *April 25, 2002*

"Hey, man, heavy shit, man…are we drivin ok, man?"
—From the film *Up in Smoke*, written by and starring
Cheech Marín and produced by Lou Adler, 1978

More than forty years after César Chávez began organizing
farmworkers in California, the word depicting that struggle
for justice has been sold for a million dollars.

In The Beginning

Chicano is a word that invokes the radicalization of Mexican-American politics during the Civil Rights Movement
and until recently, despised by those who prefer more neu-
tered, poeticized labels—Hispanic, Latino, Mexicano, Tejano, Hispano, Mexican-American. Chicano in the sixties
meant anti-war protests, long hair, MEChA, the Brown Be-
rets, Corky González, and La Raza Unida.

While the word defended a culture, it was a political act
to be one. I embraced this word, Chicana, in my college days
in Texas, because it was imbued with the me that was hated:
my brown face, my clumsy English and broken Spanish, my
farmworker traditions.

To me, this word is as sacred as my *abuelita's* embroidered
tablecloth. I embraced it, shaping it into my own reflection,
Chicana. With this heirloom, I could begin the difficult journey to loving myself for exactly who I was. A proud word, it
conveyed history, defiance, and finally, soul—evolving over
time into something deeper than tribe or belonging or even
loyalty to the family who sacrificed for me.

In my own way, I discovered that Chicano means true love of self, so that I could love you and all, so that I would not do to others what had been done so brutally to me.

Chicano. In our best moments, a new *conciencia* for America.

But, *ay,* the glitter of a rhinestone necklace is seductive, and there are shinier words now that have the same worth—globalization, acceptance, wealth, fame.

And so we have sold the only land we have left—our word for struggle, justice, hope.

I think we sold ourselves too cheaply. I think the price we will pay is too high.

The Sale

Now on a lavish five-year fifteen-city museum tour around the country, the word Chicano is going mainstream. Impulsed and created by the entertainer Cheech Marín's private collection of Chicano art, presented by Target Stores with the sponsorship of the Hewlett-Packard Company, Chrysler, Jeep and Dodge Brands of DaimlerChrysler, organized and produced by Clear Channel Entertainment, legitimized by the Smithsonian and applauded by cultural leaders and many of the artists in the exhibit. Chicano is coming to a city near you.

In San Antonio, Texas, where the two-pronged for-profit exhibit had its national debut, the multi-media *Chicano Now: American Expressions* which accompanies the painting exhibit *Chicano Visions: American Painters on the Verge,* was greeted with *gente decente* gratitude from the city's leaders and robust articles in the *San Antonio Express-News.* And thanks to Cheech Marín's celebrity power, *Chicano* is lavished with freeway billboards, bilingual media spots, and

opening night *pachangas* gushing with the music of Los
Lobos, accordionist Flaco Jiménez, a parade of lowriders,
cowboy boots, and invited taggers (who were reprimanded
for spraying on the corporate logo).

Highlights from the Interactive *Chicano Now!*

The political comedy troupe, Culture Clash, in a video tour
de force, guides visitors through the exhibit as the "Brown
Men," funny illegal aliens in spacesuits; "Border," with an
eye-catching quote from poet and writer Gloria Anzaldúa;
"Family," which includes a tender clip of Cheech Marín's
own *familia*; "Food," with an interactive stove that lights
up a pan of refried beans as comedian Paul Rodríguez nar-
rates the story of Mexican cuisine; "You can make a *taco* out
of anything"; An altar; a family album of Vietnam hero Roy
Benavidez; "Work," featuring muralist Judy Baca and note-
worthy people who would probably die if you called them
Chicanos; Astronaut Ellen Ochoa's spacesuit; boxer Oscar
de la Hoya's gloves; Santana's guitar; and Flaco Jiménez's accordion; "Música," a media installation of couples dancing
the *polkita* ad infinitum; "What is Rasquache?" video installation featuring jokes by Paul Rodríguez and George López
juxtaposed with cultural scholar Tomás Ybarra-Frausto's
quote: "To be *rasquache* is to be down but not out."

But keep going. There is one free-standing pillar to the
Chicano Movement besides the encased display on Chicano *literatura,* and in the middle of that there are video
performances by MacArthur fellow Guillermo Gómez-Peña
alongside Robert Rodríguez's film clips, featuring his *From
Dust till Dawn* with a half-naked Salma Hayek writhing with
a python. In the next room, *poetrical* short films by filmmak-
ers Gustavo Vásquez and Lourdes Portillo.

Cheech himself had a large role in the thematic scheme, which is a mishmash of scholarly quotes, comedy, videos, high-tech energy and sound, dioramas, murals, and the *pieza de resistencia*, a lowrider simulator, where you can climb on and cruise as Cheech's voice takes you through the *barrio. ¡Órale!*

Curated by (your guess is as good as mine) Consultant René Yáñez.

What's next, the world's largest burrito? Chicanismo is over the day this happened.
—Esteban Zul, Chicano writer and filmmaker, who owns the trademark to the word *pocho.*

This looks like a Chicano Disneyland.
—George Cisneros, San Antonio video artist.

The Artist

"Baby, you don't understand." *Chicano Visions! artista* Adán Hernández challenges my criticisms one morning over *tacos* at the Blanco Café in San Antonio. He explains how hard he has worked in the *barrio* that he comes from, how Chicano artists have been marginalized, excluded, how the museums "have kept us out…with our own tax money."

And he's right. While Chicano public and nonpublic art has been included in cultural centers, university libraries and other regional museums, national tours have been far and few between—most notably, the CARA (*Chicano Art: Resistance and Affirmation, 1965–1985*) exhibit, which, ironically, closed in San Antonio in 1993 after a tour of ten cities. That exhibit was the first major national art show organized and represented by Chicana Alicia Gaspar de Alba

in *Chicano Art: Inside Outside the Master's House.* "It con-
stituted a historic, cultural, and political event... Politically,
CARA countered the aesthetic traditions of the mainstream
art world, challenging institutional structures of exclusion,
ethnocentrism, and homogenization."

"Baby." Hernández confides as I compliment him on his
much-deserved two-page review resulting from his work
being selected for *Chicano Visions!* Cheech has asked him
to talk to me about my questioning, he says. "I'm not happy,
but what choice do we have? When we get through, the *arte*
will be there, the *arte* will be intact and pure with its idealism."

Highlights from the *Chicano Visions!* Painting Exhibit

No catalog, little text, no audio-cassettes or curriculum
guide was available in San Antonio. Gypsy Kings muzak accompanied my viewing. The admission was $8.00, a princely
sum for this area. Brassy, startling, and at times overwhelm-
ing, the exhibit included many renowned artists, including Carlos Almaraz, David Botello, Vincent Valdez, George
Yepes, John Valadez, Alex Rubio, Eloy Torres, Jesse Treviño,
César Martínez, Frank Romero, Leo Limón, Gilbert "Magú"
Luján, Glugio GRONK Nicandro, Wayne Alaniz Healy,
Adán Hernández, Raúl Guerrero, Rupert García, Charles
"Chaz" Bojórquez, Melesio Casas, and Gaspar Enríquez.

In San Antonio, artist Cruz Ortiz did a foyer installation of his Chicano pop-art that was eerily reminiscent of
in-store Target sale ads. His prints were Scotch-taped on the
bathroom stalls as well.

Now you see why Cheech and King agreed to keep
talking.

The *Chicano!* blockbuster is underwritten by a class of

corporations decades away from the beer companies that have hovered around our civic organizations (LULAC, MAL-DEF, National Council of La Raza, G.I. Forum) for decades, supporting justice with one hand and alcoholism with the other.

Go to any Target and you will not see a White person.
—Off-the-record comment by a Chicana filmmaker who knows her way around San Antonio.

It's a horrible situation, agrees Laura Esparza, the former director of the Smithsonian-affiliated Museo Americano in San Antonio, and the chief negotiator for the *Chicano Now!* Exhibit at the time. Her meetings with the sponsors and Cheech began in April of 2001, an unusually rushed timetable to assemble a show by the sponsorship projections of December in the same year. Museum exhibits generally take at least several years to design. And "the Target bullseye had to be on every piece of collateral that was in the show." Yes, it was a struggle, she says, but one that museums all over the country are making. Blaming the lack of government support for their predicament, she said that the Smithsonian is a prime example of "having to sell out." Check out the American Association of Museum Corporate Guidelines, she encouraged me. She tells me to determine what the violations in merchandising were in this case.

According to Target's latest annual report, their pre-tax profit from $30 billion dollars in gross revenues was a little over two billion dollars. They are committed to giving 5% of their federally taxable income to non-profit organizations. They are also committed to delivering a "superior return" to their shareholders, and over the past five years, they have generated a return of 44%, well above the industry stan-

dard. When I asked Douglas Kline, a Target spokesperson,
(the press releases quote marketing executives from each
sponsor) how much the company planned to spend on
Chicano Now!, he chillingly answered that this wasn't public
information. "So what percentage of your customers are U.S.
Latinos?" Same answer. When I told him that in my past life
working for an oil company I had to understand the twining
of public relations and marketing, he interrupted my next
questions, he had a conference call to get to. End of conversation.

I know they're stinkers…when push came to shove, I felt for
the artists…who had been working so long in the communi-
ty… Do I have a million dollars to mount an exhibit?
—Off-the-record anger by a principal in the *ChicanoNow!*
laberinto.

The problem is that museums need money. This past
January, over a hundred of the nation's most prominent
scholars signed a letter addressed to William H. Rehnquist,
Chancellor of the Smithsonian's Board of Regents, where
they took issue with the growing corporate influence in the
nation's telling of its history. They challenged the institution's
partnership with Fujifilm and the National Zoo, KMart and
a mobile exhibit featuring African-American music, General
Motors and the National Museum of American History, and
especially the entrance of McDonald's in the National Air &
Space Museum.

We're living in a different reality…when I've gone to foun-
dations…and you want to do a Chicano exhibit that has
content…they want smiling faces.
—René Yañez, curator of the *Chicano Visions!* exhibit and

consultant to *Chicano Now!*

"More than anything else, the Smithsonian is a repository for American history, heritage and achievements," said the scholars. They worried that General Motors would have an influence on the transportation exhibit… We will see whether the exhibit tells of industry resistance to efficiency and safety standards, and whether it recounts how General Motors was found guilty of a criminal conspiracy that destroyed local trolley systems across the country." You could almost hear the whispers of global warming, the echoes of the Middle East and the gavel of the Enron hearings as they questioned who would define the story of the American automobile.

I don't think you're being objective.
—BBH (now Clear Channel) spokesperson who refused to give me Cheech's phone number.

"This is not trivial at a time when we are, as a nation, engaged in an effort to explain and uphold our values both in our own country and across the world," the scholars concluded.

The Broker

The word "corporate" is not a dirty word to all Chicanos. Henry Muñoz, a San Antonio wheeler-dealer and recent Vice-Chair of the Smithsonian Board, the only Chicano—as he calls himself—on that esteemed perch, has visions, too. Speaking to me from the austere conference room of his architectural design firm, Kell Muñoz, a company that he co-founded and leads as CEO, he explains his trajectory

as a political fundraiser extraordinaire—though he left former Governor Ann Richard's cabinet after murky charges of
fiscal mismanagement (political sabotage, he says)—to the
epiphany that led him to his true calling in art.

Pointing to the one piece of art in the room, a photo-
graph of a stuffed black trash bag by Chuck Ramírez that
the *artista* says stands for our consumption, Henry tells me
of his past at the Chamber of Commerce, at Texas Public
Radio, the Guadalupe Cultural Arts Center. As "The Ugly
King," or *"El Rey Feo"*—when he raised the most money ever
for scholarships in the city's 1998 Fiesta Celebration. Most of
all, he is proud of his firm's prize-winning *rasquache* style of
architecture in the *mestizaje* climate that is today's Velveeta
with *jalapeño* Texas.

An elegant man who is the suburban-raised and private-
schooled son of a labor leader, he tells me that "nobody had
the political/cultural/private experience in 1995 to renovate
the historical Alameda Theatre in San Antonio." While the
city wanted to purchase it, Muñoz had a grander idea—to
bring the Smithsonian to San Antonio. By then he had
organized a non-profit corporation that would umbrella
offices, a theatre, and a museum—that given its presence in
the tourist-lode that is the city's old Market Square—would
find a permanent, and captive, audience.

The Museo Americano at the Alameda Theatre under
Henry (that's what we call him and it in San Antonio) was to
be the crucial *puente* to Cheech and BBH's crossing ambitions. The Witte Museum, the previous host of BBH exhibits,
"is trying to meet the changing paradigm," says Esparza who
has since left the Alameda to be the Program Director of the
Mexican Heritage Plaza in San José, California. The Witte
decided to pass on the exhibit, because they needed "to
make choices that are well-timed and sensitive."

In other words, says San Antonio native Dr. Ellen Riojas-Clark, who was originally invited to be part of the scholars committee, and declined the offer after not seeing the blueprints, the Witte could smell the coming controversy. "I would lead the first demonstration against it", she warned them.

BBH was a little bit confused about what they had, remembers Esparza. As she looked at the sketches of the interactive *Chicano Now!* exhibit…she realized that it "needed to be spun as an educational show—for San Antonio, it was very naive." Because the Alameda itself was not physically ready to host a show, she chose the old Kress Building on Houston Street, "across from the Buckhorn Museum and beside the Children's Museum," as she considered the tourists that would visit the show. In fact, she mentions the word "tourist" often.

Well we did not figure that BBH would play by another set of rules. It was as if the movimiento, the 1980s and 1990s did not happen. As if none of the things or progress we had already fought for and won in the museum world counted.
—Karen Mary Dávalos, Professor of Anthropology, Loyola Marymount University, Los Angeles, and one of the members of the hastily-assembled scholars committee for *Chicano Now!*

Why wasn't it called Cheech Marín's "Private Collection?" he questions. That's the way other collectors have shared their art. The why is left unanswered. Ortiz-Torres, who has been called "one of the most exciting artists in the Americas" by the *Seattle Times*, and is a curator in his own right, doesn't believe that the artists' careers will be better served by their inclusion in this show. They don't need it, he says. Unless they want to be on bank checks or corporate promotional posters.

This needed a couple of years to slow-cook.
—Joe Díaz, private collector and San Antonio Museum of Art Trustee.

Who is it aimed for? [Are we] a cartoon for the gringos to look at?
—Nino Acuña, University of Texas at San Antonio student, responding to both *Chicano* exhibits.

The Cost

At the Esperanza Peace and Justice Center where I work part-time, a Chicana superhero, Citlali, is primed for battle—every inch of her bronze skin has muscles rippling like the bullet cartridge strapped on her chest, and she is the kind of hero I've never seen before. She looks like me. Boldly painted on large canvases that evoke the Mexican revolutionary *artista* David Alfaro Siqueiros if he had been reincarnated as a contemporary *lesbiana*, Vásquez has occupied three rooms in a mixed-media installation. Disturbing, profane, familiar and inspiring at the same time, Citlali's creator, Deborah Vásquez, is an MFA-credentialed Chicana who realizes that her work may never be in a major museum. Too in-your-face-*cabrona*-kind-of-stuff. Though I can tell that she wants her art to be seen, valued, remembered. The essential battle of our collective politics and personal ambition requires that we be more than merely human, but divine, warriors. And who is that?

I met with the BBH and the Target people…[I] was very

respectful but you should do it the right way.
—Vincent Valdez, the youngest *artista* in the *Chicano Visions!* exhibit.

Though Citlali is trying hard. While praising the artistic quality of the painting exhibit, Vásquez told the *San Antonio Express-News* that the *Chicano* exhibits "were an effort to make Chicano culture palatable to the dominant culture… the whole purpose of Chicano art was to raise consciousness, so people would leave the exhibit saying they wanted to change things… Chicano art was always meant to ignite the flame for our youth so they could make this a better place to live."

"Now we are the *pinche* targets," Vásquez tells me later in disgust. There was some twisted consolation. Cheech Marín had scribbled "Hi, Babe!" on her napkin thinking she wanted an autograph when Vásquez tried to talk to him.

We have to take the devil's money to do God's work.
—Off-the-record Chicano museum executive.

The Defeat

"I love that Cheech wouldn't waver," says the *navaja*-tongued Richard Montoya, one of the Culture Clash comics, defending the contradictions of what he says on stage and working for the corporate enemy at the same time. "In the big picture, I love that the word [Chicano] is out there… Target and Clear Channel would have loved it if it [was] called Hispanic." So the scholars have problems with the exhibit, he whines a stuffy imitation. "Academics have been shutting us out for years. It's bloody hard to do what he does," he explains, "the life of a cutting-edge *artista* is not for the meek.

The word [Chicano] is getting some more mileage, the immigrant trying to cross, we're being subversive."

So I didn't like the opening night? *Al contrario*, he was
gratified. "The lines, the *gente*, the families…when the show
goes to D.C., it will be free, it will be closer to the epicen-
ter…it will have to change and improve."

"Look," says the flamboyant emblem and comedic voice
of resistance to a generation of Chicanos: "We are in the
ghost-dance days of Chicanismo."

Writing about the Chicano Movement and its intimacy
with art in 1980, Montoya's uncle, Malaquías Montoya,
described Chicano art as developing out of "this social and
political movement." The Movement in the late 60s, he explained, made it possible for Chicanos to look…away from
the required assimilation process that was to have enabled
them to become "something better." Artists were seen as
important to the Movement, he said, and it began to have a
powerful impact.

That's true. My state of Texas does not look like the
same state I was born in, thanks to the changes the Chicano
Movement engendered. For the first time in our history,
a Spanish-surnamed businessman, Tony Sánchez, is the
Democratic candidate for Governor. Victor Morales, a high
school teacher, made the Democratic primary for the Senate
against Ron Kirk, the Black mayor of Dallas. Ed Garza is the
Mayor of San Antonio. But much is still the same. One-third
of us drop out of high school, and for a state that is one-third
minority and growing, we may very well impoverish Texas,
given the institutionalized barriers to education that our
conservative leaders still refuse to acknowledge—and refuse
to pay taxes for.

Perhaps that's why *Chicano Now!* and *Chicano Visions!*
haven't demonstrated the spike in attendance that might

be warranted given the unprecedented publicity in all the media. Or maybe it's because of the cost of admission—a high (for San Antonio) of $8.00—to the Museum of Art for *Chicano Visions!* And $4.00 per person (including children) for *Chicano Now!* (The fees were dropped for the latter in March).

Though the exhibit opened in time for Christmas vacations, the school children began to visit *Chicano Now!* in packs of fifteen-minute tours in late February. Artist and art teacher Terry Ybáñez de Santiago, who is writing the educational curriculum, complained to me about the extreme deadline she was under last year—a project that she still hasn't finished. The kids love the *Chicano!* exhibits, she told me. "They really learned a little bit more about who they are," and considering the illusion of diversity that is Texas, she feels any discussion of identity is a good thing.

"Chicanos cannot claim to be oppressed by a system and yet want validation by its critics as well as by the communities," wrote the older Montoya continuing in that same 1980 paper on the inextricable ties between art and social change. It will be a victory, he challenged, "when Chicano communities find Chicano artists a success because they are viewed as spokespersons, citizens of humanity, and their visual expressions viewed as an extension of themselves."

Is the Chicano Movement over? Richard the actor, and the heir to the Montoya political dynasty, repeats my question. "There's only a few of us holding the banner," he answers, and "it is grinding to a halt."

Corporate identity? He laughs. "You know what concerns me?" he repartees faster than Zorro himself.

"Thirty Palestinians killed, 22 Israelis."

The Last Days

"Could it be that the same system which was opening its museum doors and at the same time planning the overthrow of Allende in Chile has changed?" continues his uncle in that 1980 article that seems so prescient today, given the Middle East conflicts and our war in Afghanistan. "Or was it the artists who started to change? Had Chicano artists really not understood that the system that supported apartheid in South Africa and at the same time provided funds for the advancement of Chicano liberation had something up its sleeve?

"A system that feeds with one hand and strangles with the other?"

"Baby." Adán Hernández, the gangster-painter with the Koolaid-green eyes listens to my arguments patiently while he smokes a cigarette. "The other alternative is nothing… I want my share of the American dream."

Maybe that's the nightmare in all of this. After all the marching and shouting and rejections, did we just want to be included in a dream that someone else dreamed for us? And is it possible to say we are different when we are just like everybody else at the same time?

Or is it possible that we have forgotten how to dream after all?

I have now arrived…Target is behind me.
—Michael Marínez, queer activist-artist from San Antonio who lives in New York.

Off-the-Record For-the-Record from the Battlefield of *Chicano!*

Using the term Chicano, it's resistance, subversion, revolution.
—Dr. Josie Méndez-Negrete, UT-San Antonio sociologist and activist.

Sanitized politics is better than no politics.
—Dr. Jorge Negrete, UT-San Antonio Professor of Chemistry and former union activist in California, married to the above.

Cheech wanted to curate it...René Yáñez did the best he could [with what was given him]. Curating by size.
—Art scholars.

I told them about the misspellings.
—Security guard Richard Ramírez responding to my criticism of the Spanish language typos at the San Antonio Museum of Art.

Being women of color, being gay, leads itself to living out of the box...instead of being ambitious you can be generous about your passions. The hope for the movement today rests with us.
—Various women and queer activists.

For the audience that Target wanted to reach...it was a slap in the face.
—Museum executive.

My hands feel a little soiled, but they're not bloodied.
—Richard Montoya, Culture Clash.

Target hates my guts..they caught me shoplifting. I can't go back.
—Esteban Zul, writer and filmmaker in Los Angeles.

*I don't think presenting this [Chicano Visions! exhibit] without
a catalog…is important.*
—George W. Neubert, San Antonio of Art Museum Director.

*If artists are corrupted by money, then I would like a chance at
getting corrupted.*
—Artist César Martínez, in a public discussion of *Chicano
Visions!*

The public will respond to what they respond to.
—Cheech Marín, when asked if the corporate sponsorship
will influence Chicano identity?

So are we the noble savages now…we're alive!
—Eduardo Jiménez, doctoral student and writer, responding
to the opening night *pachanga* and painting show.

*All Chicanos are Mexican-American, but not all Mexican-
Americans are Chicanos.*
—Who said this?

*You know it breaks my heart to see the word monopolized…
who gave Cheech the right? We're still struggling…we don't
have to sell out like we did in the 70s…like Cheech did—the
drug scene.*
—Leticia Renaud Pérez, my sister, and recovering addict.

Coming to a city near you: Next stop, Washington D.C.
on the *Cinco de Mayo* weekend, at the Smithsonian Arts &
Industries Building.

VII.
FORGET THE WAR, SO WE CAN REMEMBER IT

DEAR JOHN,

On my way to a Buddhist retreat
you on your way to the Persian Gulf

We meet on the plane
and I half-fall in love with you

Because you are reading
with one hand while the other

caresses your Mexican son

who looks like

me.

It is so much easier to
fight for peace

if I don't know anyone
like you.

Who makes war so tenderly.

You invite me to dinner
and we laugh and play

Eating artichokes, ordering mariscos
spilling secrets

Like the red wine on the tablecloth

Making peace
about the war

Churning
in our hearts.

I'll never forget you
warning me about the Holocaust

With your German last name

And the dream you had about
the jungle turning into the sea

And you and your hijito
clinging to the freighter

Last night I had a dream

That you saved me from
a raging river

After I asked God
why I had met you

And now I understand
that I am supposed to

hold on
to you

Because what you
have done

with guns
I have done with

words,

Dear John.

The Cantina at the Alamo

LatinoUSA • Apr 2004

"It was the role of a lifetime," my sister said. To play a *cantinera* in the Alamo movie with Billy Bob Thornton! Three days of walking among stars! Her name in lights!

"Honey, looooook! The Alamo!"

Say the tourists, most of them White, sweaty, cameras bouncing, capturing that Kodak moment of a loss that was a victory.

For them.

While the Brown people walk by as extras in a movie. Except at night when the tourists get scared of the *razita* from the Westside chillin in front of the McDonald's. San Antonio is a city of two worlds—one for the tourists. Another for the people like my sister who's so excited to be noticed by the cameras for once. Action!

The Alamo is surrounded by one of the poorest cities in the country. We don't have one real bookstore downtown, not that it matters on the famous Riverwalk where we have the best *cactus-ritas* you've ever tasted! There's no light rail to get there either from the PGA golf resort the developers want to build on the Edwards Aquifer, the city's only source of drinking water. But who needs water when we drink so much *cerveza*? It's just not a skinny coincidence that we are one of the fattest cities in the country, *también*.

If I could just make a movie of the Alamo, I would have you listen to the *alma* of San Antonio, following the river that keeps calling us to the past, witness to my grandmother's Spanish morning prayers, an embroidery of iron balconies and stone walls, bougainvillea blossoming into pink-fire, seductive as the *paletas con chile* outside the old *catedral*, like the first whisperings of love, finding the accordion under the native pecan trees that saw the labor organizer Emma Tenayuca go to jail in the thirties for demanding a decent wage for my *abuelos*.

How the Alamo has divided us.

And then I would tell you about Tejano R&B jammin Tuesday nights on the Black side of town. The neighborhoods demolished, but a *Despedida* college graduation ceremony with *mariachis* and proud grandparents. While their children's children, all hues and stripes, with names like Daisy, Nadia, Xochitl and Astro, go marching to protest the current Alamo in the Middle East, jasmine flowers in their spiked-up hair.

It's like we keep trying to remember what we should be forgetting. And forgetting what we need to remember. So that the stories of our crossings and *corazones* finding each other—birthing a new language and people—are lost in that grotesque monument to death.

While my sister, *rebozo*-wrapped, long brown hair and smiling, waits in that *cantina*—a knife hidden under her skirt. Like a story that cuts to the heart.

WHY WE CAN'T FORGET THE ALAMO

NPR Commentary • Apr 4, 2002

Everyone knows that San Antonio is the most magical city in Texas. The Alamo is here, but that's not the reason the tourists come. That's only the excuse.

They come for the water, known as the Riverwalk. A dream-like green ribbon running through our city, and the reason the Spaniards were able to establish missions along its banks.

One of those missions is called the Alamo, San Antonio de Valero.

After you've seen it, *Is that all, dear?* You walk across the street to Ripley's Haunted Adventure. Up and down the neighboring stores selling coonskin caps, plastic Bowie knives, T-shirts that glow in the dark and Alamo cookies, until, thirsty and wanting something more, you are descending the stone steps for the pink *margaritas* made from the purply cactus fruit, and brassy silver-buttoned *mariachis* blooming with music like the bougainvillea under the arches of the river's many bridges.

Here, at the beckoning river.

It is the same water where the people of San Antonio, mostly Brown and poor, are gathering by way of its creeks, springs and lakes, for Sunday barbeques and picnics, listening to the accordion music spicing the air alongside the Spurs basketball commentary, six packs of *frías* and chicken *fajitas*.

And while you're enjoying the Riverwalk, I'm also walking in this city's too-few parks, remembering the stories that my friends keep telling me about the San Antonio they knew before the tourists came: before Hemisfair urbanization demolished the neighborhoods and there was a dancing salon called La Gloria, bustling movie theaters with names like *el* Teatro Azteca, and a farmer's market of fresh vegetables and a young folksinger named Lydia Mendoza.

But then the descendants of the Alamo's heroes—and believers—wanted more land. This is Texas, after all, where land is the reason for being.

San Antonio grew north, like a *quesadilla,* they tell me, folding its people into suburban development, taking the hallmarks of a city—the bookstores, the best schools, the hospital, the university, then an amusement park, farther and still further north. Far from the people who settled the river. Forgetting, they say, that the water feeding the river that they depended on—was in underground caves below their parking lots and shopping malls. Two hundred and forty miles of some of the purest water in the world.

The water belongs to everyone, my friends told the developers. Without it, the land means nothing.

But the new developers won. Bowie and Travis would be so proud.

And that's why we can't forget.

THE POPCORN WAR

San Antonio Current • *Jan 23, 2003*

For sure, I don't want buttered popcorn. It's raining winter outside and my bronchitis feels better at the movies. María and I are waiting to see Denzel's new film and my mind starts making little movies about walking the dogs, the Aztlán tattoos on a man's bicep, jazzing with Cannonball and the way that my father told me he loved me for the first time this Christmas.

María tells me that when she took the Greyhound to Atlanta the other day, a whole bunch of young men and women arrived to go somewhere. She just returned from Guatemala on a fellowship and I remember when Sister Diana Ortiz, an American nun who went to work there, testified before Congress about how she was brutally raped and tortured by the Guatemalan military. Supervised by a CIA operative.

They looked scared, María says. The new soldiers, that is.

At the HEB, there are no Dust Devil vacuum cleaner bags. This is a big problem, because I really want to clean out my apartment, it's like something is finished and something new is about to happen and I want to be extra-clean. Walking through the ultra-modern grocery store that sprouted overnight in my neighborhood, there is everything but my Dust Devil, and I hear Billy Ray telling me about his dream again, where he's looking at a philosophy curriculum but then realizes he's in a prison. Wonder why I'm so interested in figuring this out?

Later, I go to pick up Norma at the airport from some academic conference and a whole plane-load of sober-faced recruits arrive with her from Chicago, and as they race after their uniformed leader, I think about how my brothers all served in the military and how they had no choice either because we were so poor. Where are these young people hurrying to? They're going to war, Norma says, and she sighs hard. Her older brother died in Vietnam, but I remember this too late.

In Denzel's movie, he plays a psychiatrist who helps a young sailor struggling with violence, and they both discover a horrible story of child abuse. The Navy ships remind me of Honolulu, all turquoise water and miles of coral necklaces for sale and hearing forties music soft as the Waikiki air, like *From Here to Eternity.*

It was as if the war had never happened and like the days before it happened at the same time. If I'm not making sense it's that I really don't want to write this column about war, yet it's the only thing I want to write about. It's like I'm surrounded by words menacing as guns, but where are the words to push back and turn them around?

It's like I'm defeated before it begins.

At the Y, the beautiful Mandy tells me about learning to prepare a will because she's going to be shipped out any day now since she's in the naval reserves. She says that the Navy men are *macho* jerks to women, though she states this in the resigned language of women who are used to it.

Meanwhile there are volleyball games for the teenage Raisa, Joan is having a birthday party, I've been dancing to Esteban's magical accordion, and Shooty, the neighbor's gangster-*gato,* is chasing my creampuff kitten off the balcony again.

The Navy sailor in Denzel's movie had no one to protect him, and he became violent 'cause he had been violated. So what violence happened to us that we caused so much suffering in places like Chile, Uruguay, Brazil, Nicaragua,

Panamá, Honduras, El Salvador, Haiti, Vietnam, and Guatemala? Colombia? And they have forgiven us over and over.

Like I forgave my father.

And why is it that we are still dreaming of prisons? And I know that the poor dream of war because it can make them generals so they can have the power to make another war. But isn't it true that every war is supposed to make peace, but we are not at peace here, inside. Not yet.

Maybe this is just one eternal Saturday at the movies and someone is watching us on a large screen, eating popcorn. And the ending is just the beginning.

THE ANNIVERSARY OF THE CHICANO MORATORIUM

*San Antonio Express-News • Aug 25, 2000

On August 29, 1970, the largest demonstration ever organized by people of Mexican descent happened in the *barrio* of East Los Angeles. It changed my life.

Though I never knew about it until now.

Gathered to protest the Vietnam War, and the disproportionate deaths of our young men, the Chicano Moratorium Committee marked the official beginning of my generation's political activism, nationalism, and scholarship.

Three people died that August day, including the crusading journalist Rubén Salazar.

On that hot day in the Texas Panhandle, where the clouds look like pieces of chipped bones floating in the sky, I was marching, too. Oblivious. But marching. On the way to my senior year of high school.

Now the Chicano Movement has ended, many scholars say. Geraldo Rivera repeated that song to a thousand journalists at a conference in 1994. Ask most teenagers, and they don't know what to say when you ask them this question, though they do know that someone named César Chávez is a defeated boxer. And if you ask their parents who are about my age, they will tell you more about Governor George W. Bush's broken Spanish then the *violencia* that the LAPD instigated in Laguna Park on that sunny day.

The year after the protest, I entered college. Fell in love with a young man whose father, a World War II veteran, had refused to let him go to Vietnam. So college it was. The next year, I took my first class with a new Chicano professor—Dr.

Alvírez. He walked in and announced he was going to give us the other side of history—our side. In my last year of college, my adviser, Hermila Anzaldúa, pushed me toward graduate school when I wanted to be an airline stewardess. She said that the good schools were looking for good students like me.

At the University of Michigan, there was one Chicano professor who invited me to his home to meet his family. Later, in my first years of professional life, I met César Chávez, the real one, on an elevator. Most elegant man who ever shook my hand. Sat beside Vilma Martínez, a Latina pioneer at MALDEF (Mexican American Legal Defense & Educational Fund), who served as their first female counsel. Watched Dr. Blandina (Bambi) Cárdenas reach President Carter's circle of appointees. Then my best friend, Annie Treviño, decided to go to Harvard Medical School. Met others who had graduated from the law school there—one who is now running for Congress.

And then, in the midst of a thunderstorm, on a night when the Texas sky cracks into jagged, silvery pieces, I met writer Sandra Cisneros.

She gave me books. I gave her my politics.

Bone by bone, we began to put the pieces of the Chicano Moratorium together. Though we didn't know it then.

The moon is a white orchid in full bloom as we walk along the river that trails her purple house. We laugh, reminiscing about the people who've helped us. The ones who believe that serving others is the greatest thing you can do. How much we want to be like them. Why is it so hard in this country to recognize that helping yourself means nothing without helping others as well?

So what about the Chicano Moratorium? I ask her.

And then we laugh again, realizing it doesn't matter that we don't remember. Because we are here.

DADDY AND THE WAR

Previously Unpublished • 2002

Thanksgiving. And Daddy reminiscing 'bout the war again.

So proud. Three years in the Philippines. His sepia portrait in the Army uniform hanging in our Pine-Sol-smelly living room, there besides the Honorable Discharge papers in their crooked brass frame, first thing you see shining when you walk in.

And the deer antlers.

His trophies.

From the dining room, where I'm sitting beside him, they stand at attention. We can't afford turkey, but Mami's roasted chicken and fresh *salsa de tomate* with the *enchiladas* and rice is paradise. I'm the oldest of eight, and already explained to my Mexican mother and brothers and sisters about the Pilgrims over and over, but Mami reminds us we're more like the Indians.

"And where are they now?" she asks, but nobody pays attention because Daddy's talking.

Real pumpkin pie. Vietnam comes after the meal. Maybe because Ernesto, Chuy, Manny, Beto, Tony, and the others are not returning after the high school graduations. Except in caskets. But I'm just innocent enough to ask why? Their pictures hanging in other living rooms too, and I miss them, and how can I tell Daddy that Beto kissed me before he left because he knew he wouldn't come back.

Daddy wanted us to bomb the hell out of Vietnam. Said it would solve everything. "See what we did to Hiroshima? Nobody invades us and gets away with it!" My father knows about fighting. His thick farmer's hands the biggest and strongest I've ever seen, and he used them for punches re-

turning from the big war against anyone who looked at him
even cross-eyed. 'Specially someone who hadn't sacrificed
like him.

My father's family comes from the King Ranch, and
Daddy was born on our homeland, *la kineña*. His family,
way before, owned twenty thousand acres, and that's why
his grandfather was killed, and it's the reason Daddy knows
about war. The winning and the losing. We lost that one,
you see. The U.S.-Mexican one.

But. By golly! He was on the winning side this time.

Mami not impressed. She's *mexicana,* and her father's
family lost almost everything during the Mexican Revolution. One million of her *paisanos* died, ten percent of Mexico's people, in that *pinche guerra.* Cussing under her breath
so that only I can hear. "And the rest, starving. It wouldn't
have happened if the *españoles* hadn't taken all the land like
the pigs they brought with them! *¡Hijos de María Morales!"*
The way she sees it, there is a price to pay sooner or later for
stealing land that isn't yours.

And that's why my family is doomed to poverty.

Someone has to pay for the sins.

No land left. That's what brought my parents together to
their *destino* on the Texas border. Both running from the
wars behind them, wars swirling around them, like shadows
following them.

I have two brothers who served in the Air Force and one
in the Army. They didn't want to go. Jorge, at the top of his
class, bored with the stupid public school, dropped out and
stole some hubcaps. More exciting than the dumb teacher,
and he got attention besides. By that time, my father and
mother had five jobs between them and fighting all the time
because there was never any money.

Besides, Daddy wanted to go back to the land. How

could school be bad? Now war was tragedy, and what did
my brother know about it?

Then the other brother, Carlos, signed up because Daddy
wasn't around anymore to stop him.

I guess my brothers wanted to make Daddy proud,
though he never returned to see them in their uniforms. But
there were new pictures for the living room walls.

Later, I forced my youngest brother, Esteban, to join too.
Mami insisted he travel the world, and this was the only
way. To become a better man than my father, now that there
was no war in sight.

Before my mother died, my three brothers' dress greens
and blues shining in the living room, prettier to look at than
all the dime-store frames of our college degrees. Just about
everyone finished *el colegio* in my family, and sitting around
the table passing the *enchiladas* and turkey, we look like
some American dream.

Except Jorge is in prison forever. And Carlos died. The
military didn't help them get Daddy back. No. They returned, but Daddy's war is still ragin in them.

Though, now Daddy says a "secret," that he never wanted
to go to war in the first place. He's eighty-five years old, and
says its time to tell stories about war different than what
you've read anywhere.

"Never forget it, no sir," Daddy starts one holiday after
the store-bought pecan pie, his favorite. "President Roosevelt went on the radio after the bombing of Pearl Harbor,
and said that the men like me who were already active—yes
sir—that we would be serving for the duration of the war."

Daddy shakes his head, his voice scratching like that
D-Day record he used to make us listen to at night when we
were kids.

His thin shoulders tremble when we say goodbye that

night. "The men just broke down and cried, *mijita*."

War is fear and loneliness, he warns. Not him, mind you, he was tough! The oldest son, his father fighting to keep him home for the few hundred acres they had left. Working, always working, sunup to sundown every day of the year. Daddy the oldest of ten. On the day he reported for duty, his father Pedro shook his hand, turned around and never looked back. *¡Adiós!*

He had work to do.

That was the last time Daddy saw him alive.

"You know what my job was in the war?" Sighting the enemy from his tank, his brown-eagle eyes aiming into the *corazón* of the target. "Isn't that something now? Fire!" Peeling the face back like a roasted onion, crunching bones into a bloody dough, crispy-crittering slanted eyes from their sockets, but he couldn't see them, don't you know? Didn't kill anyone, he just aimed. Safe as a baby in the womb, the steel-eyed cannon in front of him, President Roosevelt himself trusting Daddy's 20/20 eyes, but no one told him about the war that comes after the war. How his six sisters, panicking after their father's sudden death and the big brother's soldiering, surrendered the land he was fighting—and not killing for.

Mami used to argue that it was up to the women to stop the wars of men. That the taking of land between men was something that women knew wasn't worth the life of a son. Or the rape of a daughter. Because *las mujeres* were the ones who had to live with *la memoria* of a butterfly's wings inside them.

"Men were once *mariposas*." Though I didn't understand her then.

My mother always worrying about the women on the other side of the war. "Are they eating? What about the babies? Who will take care of the families if their husbands die?" This from the kitchen where she is making *tamales*. Mami has no quarrel with the women in Vietnam, Panama, Cuba, Chile, or the Middle East.

Only the men were her enemies.

While she was cooking and cleaning and ironing, the skinny soldiers from the Mexican Revolution returned as Vietnam veterans haunting the television news and the funerals, a war becoming a Civil Rights Movement that Zapata would have loved, she said. That war sent me to graduate school while little Black children went to jail, Mami reminded me as I packed for the University of Michigan. And because I went away, so did the rest of my brothers and sisters when their turn came.

Around the holiday table in the old days, Daddy used to talk about what a great country this is, about our God-is-on-our-side democracy. But he didn't believe that Blacks had the right to sit at the counter, though he preached we were all equal. And he knew soldiers who'd rescued the Jews in the camps. "You know what…I'll be a…there were homosexuals in there!" Didn't want to hear that women should fight alongside men. "*Las mujeres* should stay at home where they belong!" Though he was always bragging that my medals and ribbons from school proved I would lead an army.

Now, Daddy says he doesn't believe in war. Watches the news late into the night when he isn't walking around the land that will never be his. He's been writing my brother in prison for over a decade now. Tries to help us, and especially Carlos' only son, Joaquín. Think he's trying to make up for not saying goodbye at the hospital to that son who turned to drugs escaping the father he thought didn't love him anymore. Daddy never saying *te quiero, mijo*.

I don't know how it happened, but my father's war is over.

He has surrendered, finally. An old man remembering the grandfather's memories of rope coiling around an uncle's neck, and the stories before that of swords slicing open an *abuelita* from her baby, the bloody fetus dangling from his own birth cord. The gut-smoke of boots on his own father's back leaving smile-prints, cocksure grin of pistol in a cowboy's pocket. The lessons of fists closing and the *coraje* of hands slap-slapping the centuries of sons and their sons and their sons' sons reaching, finally, my face, leaving my family with so many scars you can't see for surviving the wars.

It's over. *Se acabó.* No one wins at war, Daddy says.

Esteban, the youngest, visits him as often as possible. He was six years old when Daddy left. Mami and me raising him to be different. Together, Esteban and Daddy go outside searching the winter stars, hoping to find the one, where is it, the one that is supposed to bring peace. Can you see it?

PEACE

San Antonio Express-News • *2000*

Twenty years ago I lost hope that I could change the world. After finishing a rigorous graduate program in Social Work at the University of Michigan, I went to work at a nationally prominent non-profit organization that was founded by and for Latinos. Based in Texas, I got the chance to fight for my *raza* in Washington D.C. on Capitol Hill, on issues ranging from immigration to labor to employment. I worked night and day, holidays and weekends. And loved every minute. It was the most rewarding time of my life—my great education at the service of all those people who I had left behind in the *barrio*. For my little brothers who were wasting away in the public schools. For my brother in prison who was being brutalized. For my mother with her three minimum-wage jobs that were never enough.

But my dream job didn't last. To make a long story very short, small-time, stupid corruption. The nationally-known board members preyed on the teenage secretaries. My boss accused me of teaching the young women about their right to refuse him. As one of the few high-ranking women in the place, I witnessed in-house jealousies, junkets, affairs, nepotism, womanizing politicians, womanizing bureaucrats, etc., etc., etc. Then there was retaliation for my just saying no. After four years and much crying, I left to work with the private sector, where, I figured, they know exactly what they work for: money.

For a long time, I thought that I was better than those I left behind. My ideals had suffered, but I did not succumb to the reality that my ex-boss lived by, which was "the equal right to steal just like everyone else." With my fat oil company paycheck, I spent my now-free time at Neiman-Marcus, buying all those things I could never afford before—cashmere sweaters, crystal ornaments for the tree, real French perfume. And best of all, no guilt. I was living exactly as society expected of me. My mother was finally proud of me.

During this time, I only helped my family, who was always suffering from one crisis or another—something endemic to poverty. Bought presents and turkeys. Paid for graduation dinners, barbeqwues. Legal fees for a child custody case. Summer camp for a nephew. Plane tickets for my mother to visit her dying sister. Made those inevitable family loans that are never repaid. And I gave my ten percent to the Salvation Army, the United Farmworkers, and a local Latino theatre company which inspired me. I thought I was a good person. No, let's be honest. I thought I was better than most. Certainly than you.

So why was I so mad all the time? I felt manipulated, discriminated, martyred. I hated everybody: my family, who took advantage of me. The *gringos* in Dallas, where I lived, who thought I was their easy door into multiculturalism. My colleagues, who were too passive in the face of a selfish corporation. My friends, who had moved to the suburbs to get away from the kind of people we came from. I even hated my husband Eliberto who pointed out during one down-and-dirty argument after I had called his whole family peasants for watching videos throughout the Christmas holidays, that I was not perfect either!

You think reading books all the time makes you a better person? he charged. Then prove it.

It's true, more than anything, I wanted to be a better person. But I was not. I lived to yell at the supermarket checkers at the express line, cursed at the slow drivers on the freeway who got in my way. At the fools who blocked

my path as I was protesting the Gulf War downtown. For
peace in the Middle East.

Now that I look back at all of it, I'm surprised that it
took me so long to see that peace and justice is not prac-
ticed by those of us who say we want it the most.

My girlfriends would regale me with stories about the
machos at work. But they did not mentor poor girls during
the summer youth program. Instead, they fantasized about
men whose sole achievement, it seemed, was making money
to the exclusion of everything else. My Chicano colleagues
resented the White power structure that kept them out of
executive jobs—yet they called our Black colleagues "jungle bunnies" under their breath and demanded respect for
César Chávez as they high-pitched their voices in a sleazy
imitation of *los jotos*.

Everybody I knew was angry at somebody. Everybody I
knew secretly thought they were superior to someone else—
because they were smarter, richer, lighter, skinnier, taller,
more Mexican, more sophisticated, more religious. Nobody,
but nobody, ever talked about loving. Only hate. Someone
who hated them. Someone who they hated back.

I have always believed that my whole life's work should
be about helping others. But I did not understand that I
needed help too. How hate is not only in the face of those
who dragged and beheaded James Byrd to his death in Texas. Or left Matthew Shepard to die on a fence in Wyoming.
In a way, those hate-filled acts are metaphors for the way
that we've all been dragged, kicked around, spit upon, taunt-
ed for so many generations that we don't recognize how
crippled, how wounded, we truly are.

I have asked, no, demanded that *gringos* share the
wealth, as I give nickels and dimes to the poor, and resent
what I have given to my own family. I have kept count of

the lunches I've bought, the favors bestowed, the sacrifices made. Without looking at the value of a stranger's friendship, counsel, admiration, when I least expected it.

Because love wants to come out. I suspect that it's the answer to the meaning of our lives, but we are afraid. Love is free, and for that, it's terribly expensive. We would rather buy a gift to show our love than confront the beggar who stops us along the way. They have nothing to give us, or do they? If we listen to another's story, it might break our heart, and then what? We might begin to see each other as humans, equally deserving of compassion. Of love. And it might change our life.

And though most of us are starving for something we can't name, we deny this gift at every opportunity. Though it is love we want more than anything else in the world.

See, the paradox is that we can't find the love we seek until we bestow it on others. With no boundaries, distinctions, or prejudices. Has someone hurt you? Forgive them. Love them despite. What do they have that you don't? Love, probably. You want to change them? Love them.

All my life, I have wanted justice for myself. For others. Instead, I created another world that was not so different from the world that I left behind. Didn't realize that peace and justice begins at home. In my workplace, on the bus. In my bed. At the grocery store, in the school yard. Only then will it happen in my country.

And in the world.

DON'T FORGIVE ME, DON'T FORGET ME: THE GRIEF OF CARLOS ARREDONDO WHO LOST HIS SON IN IRAQ

Testimonios after 9/11
Universidad Nacional Autónoma de México, 2010

When the Marines refused to leave after telling him the tragic news, Carlos set fire to their SUV and then himself, depending on how you understand grief and rage holding a gas propane torch.

Carlos Arredondo is a handsome man, exquisitely *mestizo* in that fair-skinned way we're proud of, sculpted, lithe, with a burning grief inside him that is haunting and also very familiar. The *gringos* in the mainstream media have described him as *medio-loco*, but we Latinos know that silence is a kind of crazy, too.

Carlos speaks with an adult-learned *inglés*, a scarred, calloused, naked language of emotions, because the English words he knows cannot tell the whole story. He smiles much more frequently when he speaks his native *español*, and you can see how in another life, he could've been a movie star. But in this life, he's driven the Boston/NYC route that I've been on several times. He still deserves an Oscar for the role of a lifetime—a father's heroic journey toward peace in the name of his beloved son who didn't believe he would die.

On September 30, 2006, Carlos Arredondo spoke on a panel titled "Losing a Loved One to War," hosted at the Esperanza Center in San Antonio, Texas. Here are excerpts from that night. [The brackets are mine.]

I immigrated to the United States in the early 80s. The U.S. was pounding Somoza [in Nicaragua] with supplies and weapons and Russia was supplying the Sandinistas, so these two powerful nations in the world were picking a fight in these small nations. We're still suffering the consequences.

I came to the U.S. because I have a dream. When I cross the border in Arizona I entered as a illegal alien and [have] spent all that time in Boston these past 26 years in America. I met my ex-wife, a really good Irish woman, and let me tell you, it's [hard] being an immigrant in an Irish country…

My son pretty much was in the high schools in Boston, (Blue Hills Regional Technical School, 1999), in the military. I thought it was the safe place. They seduced him. They call it volunteer, but they cannot fool me, I'm from a third world country and I was the last member of the family [to be told] that he was being a Marine even though I'm the one who wears the pants, though my wife makes the decisions.

I told my son, you know how I feel. I don't want you to be involved in this, I'm very worried. I don't want you to get back in a body bag. I pray for you. I support you.

He served two tours in Iraq and by that time I had it. In the media I was looking and hearing, you know, how some people don't want, I want to make a difference. (My son) was struck by a sniper in the temple and the guy who killed my son is sitting in the Iraqi Parliament…

Let me tell you, by the time the Marines came to my house (with) the news about my son's death, I had already developed a post-traumatic stress knowing that other parents had buried their sons and daughters, and look at these photos (he shows an enlarged photo of American soldiers in Iraq). Give me a break. Is that disgusting? These are children.

This is how they brought my son back (he shows another

enlarged photo of his son, this time in his casket). That's not right, that's not right, just because somebody thinks that's right.

When they came to tell me about my son's death, I asked them to leave in 20 minutes. It was my birthday, they didn't even bother to tell me can we go inside? There was my 64-year-old mother who can't speak English. None of them speak to me in Spanish.

When I saw them I thought it was my birthday surprise, then I thought it was they were trying to recruit my son Brian. By the time I asked them to leave for the third time, I was already inside the Marine van with a propane gas torch.

I already had it, being in Boston (he currently lives in Florida), being treated as an immigrant. I grew up in a country where my best friend was Black, and then I'm in Los Ángeles (where he first settled), and see the Vietnam veterans begging for money?

You think I was going to allow my son to go there? And when my son got killed, they came and did whatever they want. When this happened, Bush was in Hollywood, Florida, August, 2004, trying to get re-elected. I heard gossip about how my son died. I found ten months later in an email that came from Maine how my son died, in an email. I didn't have any experience, I thought perhaps that was the process. Just recently I was invited to Camp Pendleton to receive the last information.

The last conversation I had with my son, he call me, said Dad, I hope you are proud of what I'm doing. Don't forgive me, Dad.

Oh my God, how can I forgive you, he says it again. I love you, you're my son. Very proud, you're my son.

When he died, I realized, I thought, my God, he already killed somebody, he's feeling the guilt already.

If he was in America, he'd be with his mind destroyed,

his heart torn apart because how normal is it to kill another human being? How can they take our sons and daughters to be killers for something they cannot handle it?

I never speak in public.

Carlos has been traveling nationally. He's been to Waco with Cindy Sheehan, and showed us photos of his truck with a real casket draped with an American flag in the truck bed that he's parked at the Capitol.

I came out a year later, after my son died, and the reason is that last year I had a conversation with my ex-wife who told me that she spoke to Alex before he went on his second tour to Iraq, he was home: "Mom I don't want to go back, want to stay with the family." It was like a knife in my back because I'm responsible, I feel guilty for not doing anything about it.

Thank God I had an open casket because I got to say to my son, I'm sorry for not doing nothing about it. Remember my son sayin: "Dad, don't forget about me."

I don't forget and want to honor my son. If, let me tell you, we have thousands more than the number who died on September 11, so if 9/11 was a revenge, let me tell you, payback is more difficult for all of us.

You might only know number—my son was 968 killed in Iraq.

[Lance Corporal Alexander Arredondo of Randolph, Massachusetts, died at the age of 20 years, 20 days, and was one of the first Marines entering Baghdad. He was on his second tour when he was killed by a sniper. Carlos' remaining son, Brian, has been contacted by the National Guard.]

VIII.
LAS NALGAS
DE JLO/
JLO'S BOOTY

TWILIGHT OF THE SUMMER SHARE

To Pablito, who helped me remember

At seventeen my mother
surprised
me with a swimming pool party.
The boys chased, threw me in the pool, my
bikini pink polka dots, the girls jealous, everyone
ate bean burritos, there was even a fight
over me, I started it.
Yes, I remember.

Just turned sixty, my mother dead ten years.
Drank herself to death.
I have no daughters,
no swimming pool,
no one to admire me swimming
I'm a party of one,
remember.

Summer's over, twilight, and time for jumping
in the pool, how old am I, how
young?
The water's
cool.
It's my birthday. Don't forget.

My Picture as a Calumnista

Previously Unpublished • 2000

Ay, the miracle of makeup. And Susan Yerkes, who just
happened to have a purseful of Clinique samples when
I arrived all late for the shoot, bare-faced and dressed to
go hiking. The shade is soft honey (in the *mero*-middle of
the color spectrum, I've been told), and I'm hoping Juan,
the photographer, will make me look so good you won't
recognize me in the street. Anyway, I hide behind my new
retro glasses with the rhinestone tulips, the ones that Sandra
Cisneros gave me because she said I looked like, well, a
columnist. Boring.

While Juan pushes and prods me to tilt this way and
that, I think how ridiculous this whole thing is. Here I am,
a 47-year-old woman in the full bloom of middle-age—and
it's like the senior picture all over again. Thirty years ago,
it mattered to me that you would think me pretty. Now I
don't care what you think. I know I'm pretty. And I know
how little it matters when I sit before this laptop. How it has
nothing to do with the words that I pick, arrange, compose,
offer you like a gardener would her prized tulip. My words
are my tulips.

But this picture. Susan and my editor, Linda, are discuss-
ing how their forehead wrinkle right-between-the-eyes is
getting bigger, and I can't hear the rest. But I think they are
worried about how stupid I am looking on the computer
screen flashing my pancaked face seconds after being photographed. To pass the time, I make jokes about how much
better I'm going to look than Carlos Guerra. You know that
no way in hell is he going to wear makeup.

I think about how all my girlfriends are so beautiful, but

they don't believe it. Not really. Some of them are depressed about getting older, about menopause, and the fact that men prefer younger women than us. I see the way the women at the downtown YMCA hide their bodies, ashamed of their *mijito* scars and jiggly *panzas*, their droopy *chichis* from the years of breastfeeding and husbands who wanted their *tortillas* heated at the same time. Then traffic-stopping-dangerous-curves Cristina walks into the Y, talking politics and books, and she doesn't know she could be the next Carlos Guerra one day. If she wasn't so beautiful.

I tell her that men are scared of smart women. And one who is brainy and *bella* doesn't have a chance. Just look around. That's why most of my friends have picked one over the other. Beauty is a paradox, you see. We are born beautiful, but we can't discover our eternal, bone-crunching, heart-stopping, fire-engine *sirena* wisdom with superficial diets, exercise, expensive makeup, or by demanding that men tell us how beautiful we are every minute.

Beauty comes from deep, go deeper, inside. And it has taken me all these years to find it. I found it in books. Not television, not Oprah. Not soap operas. Not cheerleading. Not day spas and liposuction.

Books. And more books. The paradox is that finding our beauty on the inside can make you more beautiful on the outside. And then you don't care what the world thinks of you anymore, because you have finally fallen in love with yourself. Finally.

Why do columnists have to get their pictures taken? Believe me, the reporters aren't impressed, and many of them work much longer on a piece than I do. Tell me the truth, do you really care what I look like? Larry, the publisher of this newspaper, said when he met me at the Christmas luncheon that I didn't look like my other picture. I think he meant that as a compliment, but I wasn't flattered. He looked just like I expected: Tall. Important. White.

Now, if Larry had told me that he loved or hated my columns, then I would have felt like Miss Universe. If I can write the words that will make you scream, shout hallelujah, *hermana*, or want to kill me with my own pen, then I feel downright gorgeous.

So forget this picture once and for all. Imagine me all sweaty after Veronica makes me jump across the bench sixty times at the Y. Or in my cheap flannel *piyamas*, all *huangas*, pockmarked with lint and cat-clawed, that I wear for sleeping, and all day when I'm writing. Or in that *mamacita*-red silk, excuse me, is that a dress? that I wore to the book fair last year on the coldest night of the year. When I surprised everybody. Especially myself.

I am not the woman you see in this picture. And if you do recognize me walking down the street, please look the other way.

Todas Somos Gloria:
The Story of Gloria Trevi

RUMBO Newspaper • Sep 23, 2004

Author's Note: Gloria Trevi was a super-famous, beautiful Mexican singer who was sexually abused by her manager and used to throw her panties at her audience in a show of utter girl-power.

It is true that war in Iraq and President Bush's Vietnam record is more important than her.

There is shameful poverty in Mexico, and thousands of dirty children are sleeping on the street and there are neighborhoods built from the trash of others. Corn *tortillas* are now imported, and the Monarch butterflies are disappearing.

Yet, we can't stop talking about her.

Gloria Trevi. The Mexican sex-goddess who almost single-handedly ushered in a new feminist consciousness— rocking Mexico more than any earthquake or volcano with her pantherian tights and sexuality—has been acquitted. The almost-nude poster child for women's freedom won't be facing charges of corruption, kidnapping and the rape of minors in her care while she was singing and satirizing virginity.

It is her manager and father of her child, Sergio Andrade, star-maker and toad-prince, who kissed and much much more the teenage stable of girls who wanted to be just like Gloria. But only she became a princess. Only she has emerged from prison ready to star in a soap opera about her life. Ready to sing.

La Trevi, as she is known, scandalized us before she and

the pedophile-producer Andrade escaped with his teen-age entourage to Spain, then Argentina, before they were captured in Brazil. In Mexico, *La Trevi* was known for her panty-throwing episodes and man-whipping on stage. She stripped Raúl Velasco of his glasses and when her TV show was at risk—pretended to slice her wrists. I was shocked, ashamed, disgusted, repulsed. But I kept reading about her. My girlfriends bought the tell-all books about her.

Yes, we talked about her more than the war.

Because she is the war we are familiar with.

You see, we too were once little girls like Trevi when she showed up in Mexico City with star-glazed eyes and a hungry heart—and met Andrade. Most of my friends, like Trevi, had fathers who weren't around for guidance when they were thirteen—the age of dolls and boys all at once. This is the critical time when a girl needs guidance about sex and love from a father, but too many of us have had milder, weaker shades of Andrade. Many of us have been molested as young girls. It is a story common as soap opera. Some of us have been abused—and a few others horribly raped—by fathers or brothers. The rest of us have just been ridiculed, ignored, degraded.

It doesn't stop us. We survive, becoming teachers, lawyers, doctors, movie stars. Get married. Some of us are journalists or columnists. You can't tell by looking at us. Too often, we won't tell you what happened, in the way that Trevi won't confront what Andrade did to her.

Well, I watched how Trevi fought back. She took the stage and dominated men the way they have dominated us. And look at how much attention she got in return. When you're a teenager, all that fame seems like love. It's not our father, but it's love. Power. We think.

And we perform, too, on our own smaller, public stage.

We pretend to be independent. As we depend on men for approval or money. We pretend to be the mistress of our bodies—while we're a sexual servant in the bedroom. Anything to please men. Tweezing and creaming and coloring and repackaging ourselves, we try to look beautiful as Trevi, hoping to be the woman that men want. If that's what it takes for a man to love us.

On this smaller stage, we talk and talk, just like Trevi. But we have been silenced by men backstage, just like Trevi. Because we are afraid to tell the truth.

And what do we have to say? War and poverty, the price of *tortillas*? For us, all that is the same tragedy as Gloria Trevi. We recognize the lonely woman so completely battered and tortured by a man that she has his child, because she wants to love and be loved in return. Yes, Trevi embarrasses. She is a glorified slave to men. And like so many, she has been humiliated, manipulated, victimized, a prisoner of the war against women in a conquered country. In a continent hammered by the fists of empire. Where even the butterflies are dying.

On this stage, the people obey, but pretend to be free.

SELENA AND CISNEROS

San Antonio Express-News • *May 28, 1995*

She died too young. He is too young to lose. Our beloved Selena and Henry are under attack—one in death and the other in life. *Así es el destino.*

We Latinos are obsessed with Selena Quintanilla, the late Tejano pop star, and Henry Cisneros, the HUD secretary. And why not? They crossed borders and put us on the map: She, Selena, the beautiful black-lace bra vixen made our music famous. He, *el* Henry, the political *catrín*, is the Texan prince who ascended to the White House Cabinet.

Two idols. A woman. A man. When Selena died, I heard people call in to the talk shows and compare her, in their grief, to *la* Virgen de Guadalupe, Mexico's patron saint. She was no less than JFK, some said, a "good girl," the fathers of the teenage fans would add—a "role model for young girls."

While I believe Selena deserves her fame, I do not see her as a Latina idol. With her burlesque-queen image, Selena manipulated her popularity with the fantasy of the virgin-whore. Look at me, her image beckoned. But don't touch. Daddy's watching.

If our female idol is a good girl who looks bad, then our male idol is a bad boy who looks good. And while Henry has been a spectacular *político*, he is no idol either. He's in big trouble for the financial ramifications of his *machismo*—he may have lied to the FBI about payments to his former mistress, Linda Medlar. And though it was his confessed involvement with her that forced him to drop out of politics in San Antonio, everyone knew. But the people protected him. "He's a man," they said. "He'll come back. There's the adultery vote, and that's a lot of votes," said the men with a smirk.

It seems to me that we idolize Selena and Henry so much because they personify the myth of our ideal woman and man. She was the 23-year-old mother who will not abandon us. Indeed, she was cherished for her Tejano pride and innocence. He is the playboy who conquers women as the men cheer and the women fall. She is rich, but is taken care of by her family. He is not rich, but takes care of women as if he were. She barely has a high school education. He went to Harvard. She is so beautiful. And he is smart. She was like a virgin. He is definitely not.

Both are extraordinary people. And if we have made idols of them, it is not their fault, but ours.

If a culture can be defined by its idols, then it is time for us to find new ones. Selena is not a Sor Juana Inés de la Cruz, the genius of Mexico. Henry is no César Chávez. Like *luciérnagas*, we have been hypnotized like lightning bugs at the media's celebration, and allowed our hunger to be important to define us—instead of defining what is really important to us.

Both Selena and Henry have paid dearly to be the idols that we have made of them. They are victims of a tragic love story—ours.

Because we have loved them too much.

Selena, sheltered by her family, didn't see that her assistant, Yolanda Saldívar, loved her with the kind of desperation that kills. Henry, surrounded by the *vatos*, didn't realize that he could be destroyed by love.

Maybe if we really believed in who we are, we wouldn't depend on others to make clay images for us to worship.

Maybe you and I are the idols we've been waiting for.

Las Nalgas de JLo/ JLo's Booty

RUMBO Newspaper • Aug 17, 2004

They are *soooo* big. And round, two halves of a Brown world.

A whole country can stand on them, dance *salsa* all night and never get tired.

They should be insured they're so fine. I think they are. But they're just *nalgas*. I have them too.

And that makes me mad. Because of those *nalgas*, perfumed, poured into silk or blue jeans, JLo is the kind of idol we have for young girls today. She's on the cover of magazines, a hip-hop artist, a movie star, she's sampled men like Michoacán ice cream cones: P. Diddy, Ben Affleck and now Marc Anthony. Isn't she what we want? Tell the truth!

Beautiful. Famous. Rich. Powerful.

Do I sound jealous to you?

JLo used to have that who's-your-mama curly black hair until after she played the late Tejana singer Selena, and the studios noticed that Latinas went to the movies—and had booty.

But JLo says that her father's people are from Europe, so where did her hair, now Barbie-dolled and straightened, come from? Guess those *nalgas* came from Germany too…

Beautiful? JLo had even more *wátchate*-bus-without-brakes! curves, until Hollywood slenderized her to 121 pounds on a 5'6" frame. As a professional dancer, JLo exercises with a vengeance few of us can match. Maybe that's why she devours men—she can't eat. I'm her height and slender too. But the last time I weighed so little I was fourteen. Now I understand.

Rich! I do like her style. More is more, and we Latinas understand that. But I have girlfriends who make grown men cry with their clothes from Target, the sales racks at Neiman's Final Call, and the flea-flava of *la pulga*.

Powerful. What to do with it if you've never had it? Can *nalgas* save that little boy in Guadalajara sleeping on the street? Or the girl in Dallas whose father was deported and now she can't go to college? Should *nalgas* welcome immigrants besides shaking them in the Puerto Rican Day parade in New York? Can *nalgas* talk to teenagers hanging out in the *barrio* about using drugs, asking them to turn off the television that only sells them junk? Do you think those *nalgas* might show us how to enjoy another's *nalgas*—with *respeto*?

And what can those *nalgas* tell that mother who lost her son in Iraq? The *nalgas* carrying the children born on this side and the other side of the ocean.

Could it be that we are in love with her *nalgas,* but not with her?

Are *nalgas* the American Dream?

A Brown world, desperate, dreams of crossing from one side to the other, for a chance to dance with us.

But JLo's *nalgas* aren't big enough.

A-DIOSA-TION: IF YOU MUST KNOW ABOUT 9/11

I have written columns, don't anymore. But I am not silent. I write books now, and I comment frequently online regarding all kinds of stories. And I vote, always.

A writer is someone who writes! And I know you're out there... I write this for you. *Tú. Nosotros* and *nosotras*. Because I belong to you, to this tribe. And knowing this, I realize I belong to the global tribe, too. We Chicanas/os are all over the world, and we are world-class. We are no better, or less. We are equal to all. I have learned this from books and from traveling. And from my brother who lives in Poland.

It seems that my columns were just a door to finding the real story behind the next door. And it's not like the people who own all the castles want to let me in, anyway.

So I've had to make my own castle. To say what I want. Speaking of, thank you, *¡mil gracias!* to Aztlan Libre Press for publishing this book. They are a castle like no other, our very own.

When 9/11 happened, I wrote a column about the way the tragic destruction of the Twin Towers was like the story about so many other people who lost their lands and homes in this country, including San Antonio.

The new Editor of the *San Antonio Express-News* (SA-EN) called me in. She didn't like it. I defended my column, and refused to be a drummer for our invasion of Iraq and Afghanistan—many other journalists at the time were being pushed into drumming, you see. I also refused to apologize for saying publicly that it was a shame that the SA-EN didn't have (Brown) prize-winning columnists. I was told "if you keep this up…"

Don't threaten me! I walked out.

Don't regret leaving. I do regret that I didn't write a more exquisite column about the invasions after more invasions after destructions of buildings and homes and babies ripped from their mama's wombs that comprise the history of Texas, and the before-9/11's that we are suffering because we don't know the past that is still our present.

They're just called different things. Golf courses that risk our water. Fracking in the name of finite petroleum. Cars when we should have bullet trains. Bullets when we're not in the Wild West, but maybe we are. Apartments facing the San José Mission. Good prisons and bad schools. Etcetera…

Today, I write books. I've written a novel, children's books, and am working on an adult fairy tale. And I read great literature—which inspires me. Remember this: If you want to write well, read the best. Some of my favorites are: Elena Poniatowska, Eduardo Galeano, Leslie Marmon Silko, Toni Morrison, Helena María Viramontes, Elfriede Jelinek, Chimamanda Ngozi Adichie. There are so many, and I am possessed by all of them.

You're hearing this from me: I know that a Chicana is going to win the Nobel Prize in Literature in my lifetime. Chicanas/os have won every major prize in literature already. Some of the best, like Sandra Cisneros, Norma Cantú, Celeste Guzmán Mendoza, Dagoberto Gilb, Luís Alberto Urrea, Virginia Grise, Jimmy Santiago Baca, Manuel Muñoz, Benjamin Alire Sáenz, to name just a few— have held the flames in my own hand despite an icy wind at my back. There is no way I could write anything of value without their stories in prose and poetry, showing me how to do it. Every book I've read is a miracle, a treasure, a bible of the most divine language.

Writing makes me free, fearless, suffused with so much joy I can barely stand it. Every time I write something, I emerge a little different swimming in this deep water, and less cowardly about what I discover. Sandra Cisneros used to say that you know you're writing well if you're putting down stories that make you laugh, cry, or *come*. If you're hiding, it just won't happen, can't fake it. It's like the theatre, too. Writing is my stage, and I hope you will clap a little even if there are times you want to kick me off. I promise to get better.

Regardless, my job is to keep you watching.

So I've tried to write in ways that matter—proud of writing it down, though I should've written much more and spent less time walking the dogs, but maybe not. The heart does not lie, though we lie to each other and our- selves all the time. If my writing can say anything, it's that each page took me to another and another and yet another story. What I said in a column really was just turning the doorknob into the first room of my soul's castle. I may have lost my column, but saved myself. And with this book, I'm kicking the door down.

More reading! I've learned after throwing too many pillows at the television that it can't give us the answers we are seeking. Since we watch to forget what we really want to remember.

Television can't help us love ourselves deeply, or teach us how we should answer the latest insult, and it certainly can't guide us through the tortured and ephemeral map of love.

And forgiving? Novels, poetry. Yes, they can help us re- move the thorns, which can't be found in a television series. The answers to our questions won't happen overnight, they lead to more questions, but good books can help us see we are not alone, that we are all on the same journey. Like Scheherazade's *Thousand and One Nights* of stories, good books and poetry have immense power to break open the heart and put it together again, stronger than ever, a geography of scars, a constellation of tears. It just takes a thousand and one books. So start writing yours.

Think of these *calumnas* and writings as my way of learning my story so that I could welcome myself into my own house. A house I built on my own land, with my words and music. And now you, and you, *y tú, también*, welcome to my *casita*.

¡Adiós! And, *adiosa*, too.

AFTERWORD

I am writing this as Donald Trump is about to become President of the United States. He started his campaign by accusing Mexicans—people like my mother—Mexican immigrants—as rapists and criminals in one of the vilest attacks against other people I've ever heard from any political leader. He started with us, and then went after Muslims, women, the disabled, Black Lives Matter, and kept going…

My mother, Marina, crossed the border by walking across the bridge in Brownsville, Texas in the late forties. Mexican workers were needed at the time, it was after WWII. I wrote my novel, *Golondrina, why did you leave me?*, based on her story. My mother was seeking freedom and love. She crossed many borders in her life, and expected all her children to do the same—the ones born here and the one left behind. Mami never found love, but she did learn that love can make you free. She encouraged me to speak both English and Spanish, to return to Mexico and visit our homeland, to respect all immigrants, and most of all, she taught me that there are two sides—to everything, especially the Alamo.

My mother, a nurse's aide, a woman who made the best *tacos* in the world, understood that this country is a paradox. Mami knew that America's "greatness" was built on genocide, slavery and colonialism. And she understood that she came to the U.S. because she wanted to have a chance, respecting my involvement in the Civil Rights Movement and the Chicano Movement because she wanted me to have that chance too. And she also wanted me to give that chance to others. Consider this the obligation of the bloody foundations of our greatness.

As Latinxs, Chicanxs, Hispanics, *mestizos*, we are a living paradox—the Native American children of rape, pillage. Conquest. Genocide. This is a story we must tell over and over again to the larger society, and we must explain how it is possible to forgive, to honor, to flourish, to embody the integration of all the world, because we have the whole world in our blood, in our culture. This country doesn't know our story, and it is up to us to tell it. We know it's possible to speak many languages, to know many dances. We know the pride in having curly-haired and blue-eyed cousins at the same time—but the larger society is afraid of our diversity. We must tell our story of sharing land with the people who believe it must be taken by force. This country was never meant to be White, it was meant to be something else. And we cannot repeat the mistakes and greed of the past. My Tejano father taught me this.

With this book, I want you to understand resistance, and the price of that resistance. But I also want you to love yourself so that you can love others. I hope I will not be in jail in the next decade, but who knows? You and you and you must carry on and tell our story a thousand times, in a thousand different ways until this country listens. Break their hearts wide open with your story. It is the only way to heal this country. And the world is listening, because they are here, around the circle of fire, too.

Bárbara Renaud González
San Antonio, Texas
December 2, 2016

Epigram

Then comes the naming of the midmost seers

And this is the grandmother, the daykeeper, diviner who
stands behind others: Xmucane is her name.
And they said, as they set out the days:

"Just let it be found, just let it be discovered,
say it, our ear is listening,
may you talk, may you speak,
just find the wood for the carving and sculpting
by the builder, sculptor.
Is this to be the provider, the nurturer
when it comes to the planting, the dawning?
You corn kernels, you coral seeds,
you days, you lots:
May you succeed, may you be accurate."

—From *The Popol Vuh, the Definitive Edition of the Mayan
Book of the Dawn of Life and the Glories of Gods and Kings*,
translated by Dennis Tedlock, Simon and Schuster, New
York, 1985

ORIGINAL PUBLISHED TITLES

Ay, Henry   18
"Henry C a Classic Tragedy"
Brown Men Can't Run   21
"Latinos Won't Find Success in Football"
Cerveza-Time!   27
"With Beer Company Paying the Bill, Hispanics Not Free"
Mejor Puto Que Joto   31
"Putting an End to the Chase"
Armed & Dangerous   43
"Texas Must Learn Lesson from Escape"
Los Dropouts   46
"Two Schools of Thought"
The Suntan Club   52
"Rich Bring Brown Skin New Status"
Muchachitas   55
"Uniforms, Like Fashion, Hide True Colors"
The Car Gods   58
"Our 'God' Driving Us Crazy"
Dan Morales, Affirmative Action Baby   61
"Morales Would Close Door of Opportunity Behind Him"
A Nation Addicted   67
"Admit It: U.S. a Nation Addicted to Drugs"
Los Regalos   71
"The Best Gifts are Wrapped in Love, Meaning"
We Must Search the American Soul to Find the
    Mexican Conscience   74
"In the Middle of the Unending and Unresolved
    Mexico-U.S.War"

Texas Governor, No Amigo   78

"Texas Governor No Amigo of Latinos"

Let's Party! It's 1999   85

"Nothing Should Stay the Same—If History
    Lessons Learned"

Pass The Turkey   121

"Browning the Thanksgiving Day Dinner Not Easy"

A Confession/The Priest   129

"Fathers & Brothers and Pain that Doesn't End"

Drugs in the Family   137

"Drug Family—Latino Family's Dirty Little Secret"

Pass the Salsa and la Conciencia   149

"In the Middle of the Unending and Unresolved
    Mexico U.S. War"

Blaming the Immigrant/Guanajuato, Gto., México   153

"Blaming Mexico for Immigration"

The Evangelicals, Santiago de Chile   163

"Being Different in Chile"

Regresé de Mis Viajes: Seeking Pablo Neruda,
    Isla Negra, Chile   167

"Regresé de mis viajes. Navegué construyendo la alegría.
    La casa de Pablo Neruda, Lucía y Tabo"

Gloria Anzaldúa/This Bridge We Call Home   207

"Cultural Bridges and Mixes Fill Chicana's Writing"

Peace   256

"Let There Be Peace…Let It begin With Me"

Selena and Cisneros   274

"Two Idols Under Attack: Selena and Cisneros"